MW01201683

Ninja Creami Deluxe
Cookbook for Beginners

Let this Recipe Book with Various of Frozen Sweets

Accompany You Through the Hot Summer Days

Diane Geller

© Copyright 2023 – All Rights Reserved.

The content contained within this book may not be reproduced, duplicated or transmitted without direct written permission from the author or the publisher.

Under no circumstances will any blame or legal responsibility be held against the publisher, or author, for any damages, reparation, or monetary loss due to the information contained within this book, either directly or indirectly.

Legal Notice:

This book is copyright protected. It is only for personal use. You cannot amend, distribute, sell, use, quote or paraphrase any part, or the content within this book, without the consent of the author or publisher.

Disclaimer Notice:

Please note the information contained within this document is for educational and entertainment purposes only. All effort has been executed to present accurate, up to date, reliable, complete information. No warranties of any kind are declared or implied. Readers acknowledge that the author is not engaged in the rendering of legal, financial, medical or professional advice. The content within this book has been derived from various sources. Please consult a licensed professional before attempting any techniques outlined in this book.

By reading this document, the reader agrees that under no circumstances is the author responsible for any losses, direct or indirect, that are incurred as a result of the use of the information contained within this document, including, but not limited to, errors, omissions, or inaccuracies.

Table of Contents

Introduction

Are you prepared to take your taste senses on a pleasant voyage via frozen treats? Welcome to the Ninja Creami, the ideal ally for all of your dessert fantasies! The Creami is going to change the way you consume handmade ice cream, sorbets, and other desserts thanks to its cutting-edge design and simple-to-use functionality.

Imagine that you are desiring a cool, creamy dessert on a bright afternoon. The Ninja Creami saves the day by enabling you to quickly create delicious frozen desserts. This helpful kitchen tool is made with simplicity in mind, so it doesn't matter if you're a seasoned dessert gourmet or a kitchen newbie.

There has never been a simpler way to create your own frozen works of art. The Creami's simple controls and pre-set programs remove the need for guesswork. Choose your preferred recipe, include your preferred ingredients, and then sit back and let the Creami do its magic. From traditional vanilla and rich chocolate to exotic fruit medleys bursting with freshness, the flavour possibilities are unlimited.

However, the Ninja Creami goes above and beyond what is typically found in ice cream. Additionally, it enables you to quickly prepare delectable milkshakes, smoothies, and even decadent frozen cocktails for those special events. Only your imagination can place a cap on the possibilities.

The Creami is a game-changer that injects delight and enthusiasm into your kitchen rather than just being a dessert maker. Let the Ninja Creami be your guide to frozen joy therefore, whether you're organizing a family event, a cozy night in, or simply want to treat yourself. With this lovely frozen treat buddy, get ready to enjoy every spoonful of pure enjoyment!

Fundamentals of Ninja Creami

A flexible and cutting-edge culinary tool called the Ninja Creami enables you to make a variety of delectable frozen delights in the convenience of your own home. The Creami is an absolute necessity for fans of dessert because of the following important features:

User-Friendly Design: The Creami was created with ease of use in mind. Even for beginners, operating it is simple thanks to its pre-set programmes and intuitive controls. You can choose your preferred recipe quickly, and the Creami will take care of the rest.

Quick and practical: Want something cold to eat? No issue! You can quickly prepare your favourite sweets with the Creami. Bid adieu to extended waits and retail visits. Indulgence is only a few steps away with the Creami.

There are countless recipe options available thanks to the Creami. You have the opportunity to play around with flavours and textures, whether you choose traditional ice creams and sorbets, unusual concoctions like frozen yoghurt, or even dairy-free alternatives. Create customised frozen desserts that reflect your own tastes by letting your creativity go wild.

Beyond Ice Cream Versatility: While the Creami is excellent for manufacturing ice creams, it has other uses as well. Additionally, you can make milkshakes, smoothies, and even frozen cocktails with it. It's a multipurpose device that gives your beverage menu a dash of magic.

Simple Clean-up: Nobody likes having to clean up after eating. You won't need to worry about the Creami. You may enjoy your goodies without worrying about laborious clean up after dessert because to its detachable sections and dishwasher-safe components.

On your kitchen countertop, the Ninja Creami delivers the delight of handcrafted frozen delights. It's a terrific addition to the toolkit of any dessert enthusiast with its user-friendly features, rapid operation, and limitless possibilities. So go ahead, let your imagination run wild, and enlist the Ninja Creami as your dependable partner in creating delicious frozen creations.

What is Ninja Creami?

With the help of the Ninja Creami, you can make a number of frozen desserts and snacks at home. It is made to speed up and simplify the process of manufacturing ice cream, sorbet, milkshakes, and other desserts.

With the Ninja Creami, you may freely experiment with flavours and textures to create frozen dishes that are unique to your tastes. Even individuals who are new to creating desserts can use it easily because it has pre-set programmes and simple settings.

This multipurpose device goes beyond ordinary ice cream makers. You can experiment with a variety of recipes and make unusual frozen delicacies that are out of the ordinary. The Ninja Creami allows you to express your culinary imagination with everything from traditional flavours to unusual combinations.

With its detachable pieces and dishwasher-safe components, clean-up is made simple so you can enjoy your frozen treats without the stress of time-consuming cleaning afterward.

The Ninja Creami is a great addition to any kitchen, whether you're hosting a gathering, enjoying a special treat, or seeking to diversify your dessert menu. It makes it simple for you to enjoy exquisite sweets by bringing the joy of handcrafted frozen treats right to your fingertips.

A kitchen tool called the Ninja Creami is intended to make it easier and faster to prepare frozen treats and snacks at home. It was created especially to make a range of sweets, including ice cream, sorbet, milkshakes, and more. The Ninja Creami's cutting-edge technology and user-friendly features let you enjoy homemade frozen treats without the fuss of conventional techniques. The Creami comprises of a base unit with simple controls and a strong motor. Additionally, it has a basin for freezing, blades, and paddles that combine to mix and freeze your components into a creamy, delicious consistency. Before usage, the freezing bowl is pre-chilled in the freezer. As the contents freeze, the blades and paddles seamlessly blend and absorb them.

The Ninja Creami's adaptability is one of its main benefits. You can experiment with various flavours, textures, and additives to make customised frozen desserts that are catered to your preferences. The Creami has all the ingredients you need to make your culinary dreams come true, whether you're in the mood for a rich chocolate milkshake, a fruity sorbet, or a classic vanilla ice cream.

In addition, a cookbook or recipe guide that offers a variety of mouth-watering recipes to explore is frequently included with the Ninja Creami. These recipes have been specifically created and tested for the Creami, ensuring top-notch results each and every time. However, you may also let your imagination run wild and create your own distinctive frozen dishes using your preferred components.

Benefits of Using It

Convenience: Making handmade frozen delights in your kitchen is made possible with the Ninja Creami. You don't have to rely on store-bought alternatives or go to ice cream shops. You have the ability to make delectable treats with the Creami whenever the urge arises.

Customization: The Creami's capacity to let you to create unique frozen concoctions is one of its main advantages. To fit your tastes, you can experiment with different flavours, ingredients, and textures. The Creami enables you to create individualised desserts that are catered to your taste, whether you prefer traditional flavours or wish to experiment with novel combinations.

Saving Time and Money: Using the Creami to make your own frozen desserts can save you both time and money. You can avoid the lengthy lines and high costs at dessert shops. Additionally, the Creami gives you control over the type and amount of ingredients used, resulting in a tasty and affordable dessert.

Healthier Alternatives: You can choose the ingredients that go into your desserts while using the Creami. This implies that you have the choice of selecting healthier substitutes, such as fresh fruit, dairy-free products, or the use of natural sweeteners. It is appropriate for a variety of lifestyles since you may accommodate dietary needs or preferences.

Creative Exploration: The Creami fosters culinary experimentation by providing countless options for frozen sweets. You can experiment with flavours, try out new recipes, and even come up with your own original dishes. It's a fun way to express your creativity and delight your palate with unusual pairings.

The Creami is a fantastic tool for creating enjoyable and special moments with your loved ones. Making desserts with the family, especially the kids, can be a fun pastime that promotes camaraderie and makes treasured memories.

Simple Clean-up: The Creami makes cleanup easy after making desserts. Its detachable pieces and dishwasher-safe components make cleanup simple and quick, letting you concentrate on enjoying your mouth-watering creations.

Versatility: The Ninja Creami is capable of making more than just ice cream. It allows us flexibility in producing a variety of frozen delicacies. You may make sorbets, frozen yoghurt, gelato, slushies, frozen custard, and even unusual concoctions like granita. The Creami brings up a world of opportunities, guaranteeing that there is enjoyment for everyone.

Quick outcomes: Don't want to wait for hours to get your favourite frozen treat? The Creami saves the day with its quick and effective freezing skills. You may quickly prepare the dessert of your choice, allowing you to immediately sate your sweet tooth.

You have control over portion quantities when using the Creami. In order to ensure that you may enjoy your frozen sweets in moderation, you can produce little or large batches depending on your needs. For people who are controlling their calorie consumption or portion sizes, this option is especially helpful.

Entertainment Value: Using the Creami may be a fun and interesting experience. It can be exciting and anticipatory to see the ingredients come together into a creamy frozen treat right before your eyes. It gives making desserts a fun factor, making it entertaining for both children and adults.

Impressive Presentation: With the Ninja Creami, you can make desserts that are aesthetically pleasing and can wow your guests or elevate a personal pleasure. To make magnificent presentations that appear as wonderful as they taste, experiment with various textures, layers, and garnishes.

Temperature Control: The Creami provides accurate temperature control, making sure that your frozen delights reach the ideal consistency. Depending on your desire, you can change the settings to make soft-serve or firm ice cream. Every mouthful will have a pleasant texture thanks to this level of control.

Electricity Efficient: Compared to conventional ice cream makers, the Creami uses less electricity because of its energy-efficient design. This helps you make desserts in a way that is more ecologically friendly while also saving you money on your utility expenses.

Learning Experience: For budding chefs or those curious about the science underlying frozen desserts, using the Creami can be a fruitful learning opportunity. You can improve your culinary abilities by having the chance to comprehend the concepts of freezing, emulsification, and flavour balance.

The Ninja Creami provides convenience, personalization, cost savings, healthier options, artistic discovery, family connection, and simple cleanup, among other advantages that improve your dessert-making experience. For those looking for delicious frozen sweets prepared with passion and creativity, it's a lovely addition to any kitchen.

Step-By-Step Using Ninja the Ninja Creami

Getting ready: Compile all the items required for the recipe you've chosen. Fruits, sweeteners, dairy or non-dairy bases, flavourings, and any other mix-ins or toppings you choose can be included.

Make that the Creami is correctly put together in accordance with the manufacturer's instructions. Make sure the removable components are firmly fastened and that the freezing bowl is dry and clean.

Choose a Recipe: You can choose a recipe from a cookbook, an online source, or you can come up with your own. Think about the flavours and textures you want your frozen delight to have. Choose a recipe that appeals to your taste, whether it be traditional vanilla, fruity sorbet, or a delicious chocolate concoction.

Prepare the Ingredients: To prepare the ingredients, follow the recipe's instructions. This could entail heating mixes, blending the base ingredients, or blending fruits. Make sure all the components are thoroughly mixed and that any chilling or freezing processes are carried out.

Preparation: Carefully pour the prepared mixture into the Creami's freezer bowl. Because the mixture will expand when frozen, avoid overfilling the container. Give the mixture some room to expand and circulate appropriately.

Lid Attachment: Top the Creami with the lid in a secure position. Make sure it is wrapped tightly to avoid any leaks during the freezing process.

Set the Programme: Choose the proper programme or setting for your recipe based on the Creami model. This can be a dedicated programme for sorbet, ice cream, or other frozen treats. Set the desired time and speed in accordance with the directions for the recipe if your Creami doesn't have pre-set programmes.

Press the start button to begin the freezing process, or follow the Creami's instructions to do so. The mixture will start to freeze and churn in the Creami, creating a creamy frozen dessert. Depending on the recipe and Creami model, the procedure might take anywhere from 10 to 30 minutes, so patience is a virtue.

Track the Development: Throughout the freezing process, keep an eye on the Creami. The mixture can start to thicken and swell in size. By lifting the lid, you may also occasionally check the consistency and texture. Don't forget to be close by while operating the Creami.

If your recipe calls for mix-ins like chocolate chips, nuts, or cookie crumbs, add them in the final few minutes of freezing. They can then be dispersed evenly throughout the frozen treat thanks to this.

Pause the Creami and carefully remove the frozen bowl once the freezing procedure is finished. Scoop the ice cream into dishes or cones for serving. If you'd like, you can add more toppings to the dish.

Serving and enjoying your homemade frozen dessert right

away is recommended. Transfer any leftovers to an airtight container and place them in the freezer so you may enjoy them later.

You can confidently use the Ninja Creami to make a range of frozen treats in your own home with the help of these detailed instructions. Enjoy the thrill of making your own frozen delicacies with care and let your imagination go wild.

Tips for Using Accessories

Here are some helpful hints for using the Ninja Creami's accessories:

1. Before using, make sure the freezer bowl has been well cleaned and dried. This will stop any leftover flavour or texture from earlier frozen desserts from influencing your new creation. To make sure the freezing bowl is well cooled, it's also a good idea to store it in the freezer for a few hours before using it.

2. Blades and Paddles: Use caution when handling the Creami's blades and paddles. They should be handled carefully because they are sharp. Follow the manufacturer's directions when assembling or disassembling them to guarantee a secure fit.

3. Mix-in Containers: If your Creami comes with extra mix-in containers, use them to give your frozen delicacies an extra layer of flavour and texture. Prior to freezing, prepare your mix-ins and have them available to add. This makes it simple for you to add tasty variations like

chocolate chips, almonds, or cookie crumbs.

4. Recipe Booklet: A recipe booklet or guide is frequently included with the Ninja Creami. Make sure to read it to learn about brand-new, mouth-watering recipes created especially for your appliance. Great results are guaranteed because all recipes have been tried and tested on the Creami.

5. Experimentation: Don't be scared to use your imagination and try out various flavours and ingredients. There are countless possibilities with the Creami. To produce distinctive and customised frozen delights, experiment with different fruits, extracts, or even spices. Make notes about your trials so you can duplicate your preferred mixtures later.

6. Timing and Texture: Pay close attention to your recipes' suggested timings and the desired texture of your frozen dessert. In order to obtain the desired consistency, different recipes could call for different freezing times. Reduce the freezing time slightly if you desire a softer texture; a longer freezing time will provide a tougher texture.

7. Timing of Mix-ins: Carefully consider the timing if you intend to add mix-ins to your frozen desserts. If they are added too early in the freezing process, they can sink to the bottom, and if they are added too late, they might not get distributed evenly. To ensure even distribution, according to the recipe directions or add them in the last few minutes of freezing.

8. Cleaning and upkeep: Be careful to give the accessories a thorough cleaning after each use. To clean the blades, paddles, and freezing bowl, adhere to the manufacturer's instructions. In doing so, the accessories' durability and functionality will be maintained.

You can maximise the use of the accessories that come with your Ninja Creami by remembering these suggestions. To make delicious frozen delights that will impress family and friends, enjoy experimenting with new flavours, textures, and combinations.

Cleaning and Caring for Ninja Creami

Your Ninja Creami will function better and remain in outstanding shape if you clean and maintain it properly. Here are some cleaning and maintenance advice for your Ninja Creami:

Disassemble and disconnect: Always unplug the Creami from the power source before cleaning. Disassemble the removable components with care, following the manufacturer's instructions. The freezing bowl, blades, paddles, and any other removable parts are normally removed during this process.

Hand-Washing: Use warm, soapy water to wash the removable pieces by hand. To thoroughly clean each item, use a soft sponge or towel and a mild dishwashing detergent. Pay close attention to any food residue on the blades, paddles, and other locations. Rinse them thoroughly to get rid of all soap traces.

Do Not Submerge Base: Never immerse the base of the Creami, which houses the engine, in water or any other liquid. To get rid of any spills or stains, just wipe it clean with a moist towel. Before putting the Creami back together, make sure the base is totally dry.

Dishwasher-Safe Parts: To determine which of the removable parts are dishwasher-safe, consult the manufacturer's instructions. If so, you can easily clean them by setting them on the top rack of your dishwasher. To ensure the longevity of these parts, hand washing is typically advised.

Drying: After washing, let everything air dry fully before putting the Creami back together. Make sure there is no moisture left on any of the parts because this might lead to mould growth or long-term damage. If necessary, you can also wipe them dry with a fresh, clean cloth.

Reassemble the Creami after the components have dried out, then keep it somewhere clean and dry. Avoid keeping it in humid or close to heat sources. To avoid any loss or misplacing, keep all the equipment together.

Periodically inspect the Creami for any indications of wear, damage, or dysfunction. If you experience any problems, see the user manual or get in touch with the manufacturer for advice on upkeep and repairs.

Safety precautions: When cleaning and taking care of your Ninja Creami, put safety first. Never submerge the base in water or let liquids touch it. The blades and paddles should only be handled with care as they are sharp. When not in use, keep the Creami out of children's reach.

You can make sure that your Ninja Creami stays in top shape for a very long time by according to these cleaning and maintenance suggestions. This will enable you to continue to enjoy a variety of delectable frozen delicacies while preserving the appliance's operation and performance.

Frequently Asked Questions & Notes

Can I use the Ninja Creami to make dairy-free or vegan frozen treats?

A: Using non-dairy milk or cream substitutes, such as almond milk, coconut milk, or soy milk, you can definitely make dairy-free or vegan options. There are numerous recipes that can be made to suit different dietary requirements.

How long does it take the Ninja Creami mixture to freeze?

A: Depending on the recipe, preferred texture, and Creami model, the freezing time may change. The process usually takes between 10 and 30 minutes to reach a creamy consistency. It is advised to adhere to the specified freezing times listed in the recipe.

Can I use the Creami to make larger amounts of frozen treats?

A: Depending on the model, the Creami's capacity varies. While some versions can handle larger amounts, others are made for single servings. It's crucial to verify the capacity of your particular Creami model and modify the recipe as necessary.

Can I use pre-made mixes or ice cream bases from the shop with the Ninja Creami?

A: Although you can use store-bought mixes or ice cream bases, the Ninja Creami is meant to work best with homemade recipes. Your frozen sweets will have the best flavour and texture if you use fresh ingredients and adhere to the recipe's instructions.

A: Can I make non-frozen desserts using the Ninja Creami?

A: The Ninja Creami's main use is to create frozen delights. To cook desserts or combinations that aren't frozen, some models might feature extra settings or attachments. For more details on particular capabilities, consult the user manual or recipe guide.

The Ninja Creami accessories may be cleaned in the dishwasher.

A: The Creami may be dishwasher safe for some of its removable components. For information on which components can be safely cleaned in the dishwasher, consult the manufacturer's instructions. To ensure the longevity of these parts, hand washing is typically advised.

A: During operation, how noisy is the Ninja Creami?

A: Depending on the model and the freezing procedure, the Creami's noise level can change. Due to the motor and freezing action, it does make some noise, although it is often not too loud or disruptive.

Is a light frost or condensation present in the freezing bowl normal?

A: A thin layer of condensation or frost on the bowl is normal. It is a by-product of freezing and has no bearing on the effectiveness or quality of your frozen goods.

Do frozen sweets created with the Ninja Creami allow the addition of alcohol?

A: While you can add alcohol to your frozen delicacies, be aware that doing so can lower the mixture's freezing point. A combination may become mushy or fail to freeze properly if there is an excessive amount of alcohol added. It's better to stick to recipes created especially for

alcoholic frozen delights or to refer to instructions for adding alcohol to handmade ice cream.

Can I make healthy frozen delights with the Ninja Creami?

A: By utilising wholesome ingredients and minimising additional sweets, the Ninja Creami may be used to make healthier frozen delights. You can experiment with adding fruits, using lighter bases like Greek yoghurt or low-fat milk, and using natural sweeteners like honey or maple syrup.

Can I create frozen delights without nuts or other allergens using the Creami?

A: The Creami can be customised to meet a variety of dietary requirements. Recipes and ingredients devoid of nuts or other allergens are an option. Keep an eye out for cross-contamination, and make sure that all surfaces and utensils are completely cleansed before use if you or someone you're serving has severe allergies.

Is it typical for the frozen delicacies to have a softer texture than ice cream from the store?

A: When compared to store-bought ice cream, homemade frozen delights created using the Creami might have a somewhat softer consistency. This is due to the stabilisers and chemicals that are frequently used in store-bought ice cream to retain a firmer texture. To improve the firmness of your homemade desserts, you can change the freezing duration or use recipes that call for cornflour or gelatin.

Can I refreeze leftovers or frozen desserts that have partially melted?

A: Refreezing partially melted or leftover frozen foods is typically not advised. Ice crystals may form and the texture may be harmed by refreezing. It is ideal to eat the frozen sweets as soon as they are created, or to freeze any leftovers in an airtight container and eat them quickly.

Please take note that the manufacturer's particular instructions for your Ninja Creami model must be followed. Features, capabilities, and operational recommendations may differ between versions. For comprehensive instructions and safety warnings, consult the user manual or internet resources.

Note: If you have any problems with your Ninja Creami, such as motor issues or strange noises, consult the user manual's troubleshooting section or seek support from the manufacturer.

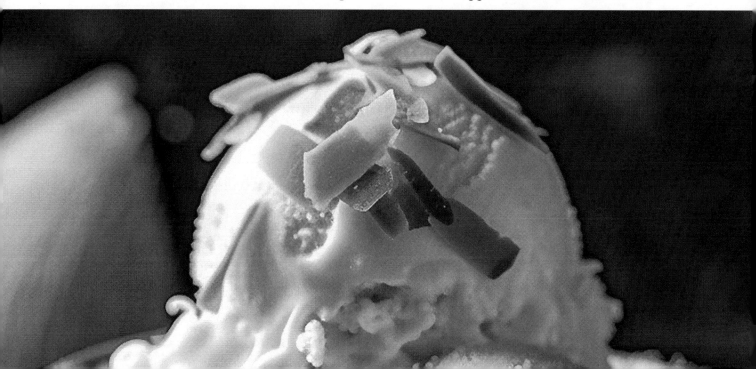

Chapter 1 Milkshakes

Easy Raspberry Ice Cream Milkshake

Preparation Time: 10 minutes | Servings: 2

Ingredients:

1½ cups raspberry ice cream   ½ cup whole milk

Preparation:

1. In an empty Ninja CREAMi pint container, put in ice cream, followed by milk. 2. Arrange the container into the outer bowl of Ninja CREAMi. 3. Install the "Creamerizer Paddle" onto the lid of outer bowl. 4. Then rotate the lid clockwise to lock. 5. Press "Power" button to turn on the unit. 6. Then press "MILKSHAKE" button. 7. When the program is completed, turn the outer bowl and release it from the machine. 8. Transfer the shake into serving glasses and enjoy immediately.

Nutritional Information per Serving:

Calories: 139 |Fat: 7.2g|Sat Fat: 4.5g|Carbohydrates: 14.8g|Fiber: 0.4g|Sugar: 13.7g|Protein: 3.7g

Chocolate Cookie Milkshake

Preparation Time: 10 minutes | Servings: 2

Ingredients:

1½ cups chocolate ice cream   2 tablespoons cream cheese, softened
½ cup whole milk   3 chocolate sandwich cookies, crushed

Preparation:

1. In an empty Ninja CREAMi pint container, put in ice cream and remaining ingredients and blend to incorporate. 2. Cover the container with storage lid and freeze for 24 hours. 3. After 24 hours, take off the lid from container and arrange into the outer bowl of Ninja CREAMi. 4. Install the "Creamerizer Paddle" onto the lid of outer bowl. 5. Then rotate the lid clockwise to lock. 6. Press "Power" button to turn on the unit. 7. Then press "MILKSHAKE" button. 8. When the program is completed, turn the outer bowl and release it from the machine. 9. Transfer the shake into serving glasses and serve immediately.

Nutritional Information per Serving:

Calories: 339 |Fat: 18.2g|Sat Fat: 8.2g|Carbohydrates: 42g|Fiber: 0.4g|Sugar: 13.7g|Protein: 6g

Fresh Blueberry Milkshake

Preparation Time: 10 minutes | Servings: 2

Ingredients:

1½ ounces vanilla ice cream

5¼ ounces fresh blueberries

3 ounces full-fat coconut milk

Dash of vanilla extract

Preparation:

1. In an empty Ninja CREAMi pint container, put in the ice cream. 2. Top with the blueberries, coconut milk and vanilla extract and lightly blend to incorporate. 3. Arrange the container into the outer bowl of Ninja CREAMi. 4. Install the "Creamerizer Paddle" onto the lid of outer bowl. 5. Then rotate the lid clockwise to lock. 6. Press "Power" button to turn on the unit. 7. Then press "MILKSHAKE" button. 8. When the program is completed, turn the outer bowl and release it from the machine. 9. Transfer the shake into serving glasses and enjoy immediately.

Nutritional Information per Serving:

Calories: 310 |Fat: 22g|Sat Fat: 19.9g|Carbohydrates: 24.3g|Fiber: 2.2g|Sugar: 17.9g|Protein: 3.8g

Vanilla Pistachio Milkshake

Preparation Time: 10 minutes | Servings: 2

Ingredients:

1½ cups vanilla ice cream

½ cup whole milk

2 tablespoons maple syrup

¼ cup pistachios, chopped

¼ teaspoon vanilla extract

Preparation:

1. In an empty Ninja CREAMi pint container, put in ice cream, followed by milk, maple syrup, pistachios and vanilla extract. 2. Arrange the container into the outer bowl of Ninja CREAMi. 3. Install the "Creamerizer Paddle" onto the lid of outer bowl. 4. Then rotate the lid clockwise to lock. 5. Press "Power" button to turn on the unit. 6. Then press "MILKSHAKE" button. 7. When the program is completed, turn the outer bowl and release it from the machine. 8. Transfer the shake into serving glasses and enjoy immediately.

Nutritional Information per Serving:

Calories: 233 |Fat: 10.8g|Sat Fat: 4.9g|Carbohydrates: 30.3g|Fiber: 1.1g|Sugar: 26.2g|Protein: 5.2g

Vanilla Ice Cream Cookie Milkshake

Preparation Time: 10 minutes | Servings: 2

Ingredients:

2 cups vanilla ice cream

½ cup whole milk

¼ cup shortbread cookies, broken

2 tablespoons cookie butter

Preparation:

1. In an empty Ninja CREAMi pint container, put in the ice cream. 2. With a spoon, create a 1½-inch wide hole in the center that reaches the bottom of the pint container. 3. Put in remaining ingredients into the hole. 4. Arrange the container into the outer bowl of Ninja CREAMi. 5. Install the "Creamerizer Paddle" onto the lid of outer bowl. 6. Then rotate the lid clockwise to lock. 7. Press "Power" button to turn on the unit. 8. Then press "MILKSHAKE" button. 9. When the program is completed, turn the outer bowl and release it from the machine. 10. Transfer the shake into serving glasses and enjoy immediately.

Nutritional Information per Serving:

Calories: 322 |Fat: 22.4g|Sat Fat: 13.3g|Carbohydrates: 25.9g|Fiber: 0.8g|Sugar: 21.3g|Protein: 4.9g

Vanilla Strawberry Ice Cream Milkshake

Preparation Time: 10 minutes | Servings: 3

Ingredients:

2 cups strawberry ice cream

1 cup coconut milk

1 teaspoon vanilla extract

Preparation:

1. In an empty Ninja CREAMi pint container, put in the ice cream. 2. Top with the coconut milk and vanilla extract and lightly blend to incorporate. 3. Arrange the container into the outer bowl of Ninja CREAMi. 4. Install the "Creamerizer Paddle" onto the lid of outer bowl. 5. Then rotate the lid clockwise to lock. 6. Press "Power" button to turn on the unit. 7. Then press "MILKSHAKE" button. 8. When the program is completed, turn the outer bowl and release it from the machine. 9. Transfer the shake into serving glasses and enjoy immediately.

Nutritional Information per Serving:

Calories: 215 |Fat: 15.7g|Sat Fat: 13g|Carbohydrates: 12.9g|Fiber: 0.3g|Sugar: 11.5g|Protein: 2.5g

Chocolate Almonds Milkshake

Preparation Time: 10 minutes | Servings: 2

Ingredients:

1½ cups leche ice cream

½ cup unsweetened almond milk

2 tablespoons roasted almonds, cut up

2 tablespoons chocolate chips

2 tablespoons shredded coconut

Preparation:

1. In an empty Ninja CREAMi pint container, put in the ice cream. 2. Top with the remaining ingredients and gently blend to incorporate. 3. Arrange the container into the outer bowl of Ninja CREAMi. 4. Install the "Creamerizer Paddle" onto the lid of outer bowl. 5. Then rotate the lid clockwise to lock. 6. Press "Power" button to turn on the unit. 7. Then press "MILKSHAKE" button. 8. When the program is completed, turn the outer bowl and release it from the machine. 9. Transfer the shake into serving glasses and enjoy immediately.

Nutritional Information per Serving:

Calories: 231 |Fat: 13.9g|Sat Fat: 7g|Carbohydrates: 23.8g|Fiber: 1.8g|Sugar: 20.2g|Protein: 4.7g

Strawberry Ice Cream Marshmallow Milkshake

Preparation Time: 10 minutes | Servings: 2

Ingredients:

1½ cups strawberry ice cream

½ cup whole milk

1 tablespoon marshmallow topping

Preparation:

1. In an empty Ninja CREAMi pint container, put in the ice cream. 2. With a spoon, create a 1½-inch wide hole in the center that reaches the bottom of the pint container. 3. Put in remaining ingredients into the hole. 4. Place ice cream in an empty CREAMi™ Pint. 5. Arrange the container into the outer bowl of Ninja CREAMi. 6. Install the "Creamerizer Paddle" onto the lid of outer bowl. 7. Then rotate the lid clockwise to lock. 8. Press "Power" button to turn on the unit. 9. Then press "MILKSHAKE" button. 10. When the program is completed, turn the outer bowl and release it from the machine. 11. Transfer the shake into serving glasses and enjoy immediately.

Nutritional Information per Serving:

Calories: 172 |Fat: 7.3g|Sat Fat: 4.5g|Carbohydrates: 22.7g|Fiber: 0.4g|Sugar: 18.4g|Protein: 3.8g

Homemade Chocolate Cookies Milkshake

Preparation Time: 10 minutes | Servings: 2

Ingredients:

1 cup chocolate ice cream
1 cup milk

2 small chocolate cookies, crushed

Preparation:

1. In an empty Ninja CREAMi pint container, put in the ice cream. 2. With a spoon, create a 1½-inch wide hole in the center that reaches the bottom of the pint container. 3. Put in remaining ingredients into the hole. 4. Arrange the container into the outer bowl of Ninja CREAMi. 5. Install the "Creamerizer Paddle" onto the lid of outer bowl. 6. Then rotate the lid clockwise to lock. 7. Press "Power" button to turn on the unit. 8. Then press "MILKSHAKE" button. 9. When the program is completed, turn the outer bowl and release it from the machine. 10. Transfer the shake into serving glasses and enjoy immediately.

Nutritional Information per Serving:

Calories: 189 |Fat: 7.4g|Sat Fat: 4g|Carbohydrates: 24.8g|Fiber: 0.6g|Sugar: 16.9g|Protein: 6.1g

Cinnamon Almonds Milkshake

Preparation Time: 10 minutes | Servings: 2

Ingredients:

1½ cups vanilla ice cream
½ cup whole milk
2 tablespoons honey

¼ cup almonds, chopped
¼ teaspoon ground cinnamon
Pinch of ground cardamom

Preparation:

1. In an empty Ninja CREAMi pint container, put in ice cream, followed by milk, honey, almonds, cinnamon and cardamom. 2. Arrange the container into the outer bowl of Ninja CREAMi. 3. Install the "Creamerizer Paddle" onto the lid of outer bowl. 4. Then rotate the lid clockwise to lock. 5. Press "Power" button to turn on the unit. 6. Then press "MILKSHAKE" button. 7. When the program is completed, turn the outer bowl and release it from the machine. 8. Transfer the shake into serving glasses and enjoy immediately.

Nutritional Information per Serving:

Calories: 273 |Fat: 13.2g|Sat Fat: 5g|Carbohydrates: 34.9g|Fiber: 2.1g|Sugar: 31.5g|Protein: 6.3g

Vanilla Oreo Milkshake

Preparation Time: 10 minutes | Servings: 2

Ingredients:

1½ cups vanilla ice cream
3 Oreo cookies

¼ cup whole milk

Preparation:

1. In an empty Ninja CREAMi pint container, put in ice cream, followed by cookies and milk. 2. Arrange the container into the outer bowl of Ninja CREAMi. 3. Install the "Creamerizer Paddle" onto the lid of outer bowl. 4. Then rotate the lid clockwise to lock. 5. Press "Power" button to turn on the unit. 6. Then press "MILKSHAKE" button. 7. When the program is completed, turn the outer bowl and release it from the machine. 8. Transfer the shake into serving glasses and enjoy immediately.

Nutritional Information per Serving:

Calories: 191 |Fat: 9.1g|Sat Fat: 4.5g|Carbohydrates: 24.1g|Fiber: 0.8g|Sugar: 18.2g|Protein: 3.5g

Marshmallow Milkshake

Preparation Time: 10 minutes | Servings: 2

Ingredients:

1½ cups vanilla ice cream
½ cup coconut milk

1 tablespoon marshmallow topping

Preparation:

1. Place ice cream and milk in an empty CREAMi™ Pint. 2. Arrange the container into the outer bowl of Ninja CREAMi. 3. Install the "Creamerizer Paddle" onto the lid of outer bowl. 4. Then rotate the lid clockwise to lock. 5. Press "Power" button to turn on the unit. 6. Then press "MILKSHAKE" button. 7. When the program is completed, turn the outer bowl and release it from the machine. 8. Transfer the shake into serving glasses and sprinkle with marshmallow topping. Enjoy immediately.

Nutritional Information per Serving:

Calories: 243 |Fat: 19.6g|Sat Fat: 16.1g|Carbohydrates: 20.8g|Fiber: 1.7g|Sugar: 17g|Protein: 3.1g

Tasty Mango Ice Cream Milkshake

Preparation Time: 10 minutes | Servings: 2

Ingredients:

1½ cups mango ice cream

½ cup full-fat coconut milk

Preparation:

1. In an empty Ninja CREAMi pint container, put in mango ice cream, followed by coconut milk. 2. Arrange the container into the outer bowl of Ninja CREAMi. 3. Install the "Creamerizer Paddle" onto the lid of outer bowl. 4. Then rotate the lid clockwise to lock. 5. Press "Power" button to turn on the unit. 6. Then press "MILKSHAKE" button. 7. When the program is completed, turn the outer bowl and release it from the machine. 8. Transfer the shake into serving glasses and enjoy immediately.

Nutritional Information per Serving:

Calories: 223 |Fat: 17.2g|Sat Fat: 14.4g|Carbohydrates: 14g|Fiber: 0.4g|Sugar: 11.5g|Protein: 2.7g

Chocolate Liqueur Milkshake

Preparation Time: 5 minutes | Servings: 2

Ingredients:

2 cups chocolate ice cream

2 tablespoons vodka

2 tablespoons chocolate liqueur

Preparation:

1. In an empty Ninja CREAMi pint container, put in ice cream, followed by chocolate liqueur and vodka. 2. Arrange the container into the outer bowl of Ninja CREAMi. 3. Install the "Creamerizer Paddle" onto the lid of outer bowl. 4. Then rotate the lid clockwise to lock. 5. Press "Power" button to turn on the unit. 6. Then press "MILKSHAKE" button. 7. When the program is completed, turn the outer bowl and release it from the machine. 8. Transfer the shake into serving glasses and enjoy immediately.

Nutritional Information per Serving:

Calories: 227 |Fat: 7.1g|Sat Fat: 4.5g|Carbohydrates: 24.3g|Fiber: 0.5g|Sugar: 22.2g|Protein: 2.3g

Classic Strawberry Ice Cream Milkshake

Preparation Time: 10 minutes | Servings: 2

Ingredients:

1½ cups strawberry ice cream   ½ cup whole milk

Preparation:

1. In an empty Ninja CREAMi pint container, put in ice cream, followed by milk. 2. Arrange the container into the outer bowl of Ninja CREAMi. 3. Install the "Creamerizer Paddle" onto the lid of outer bowl. 4. Then rotate the lid clockwise to lock. 5. Press "Power" button to turn on the unit. 6. Then press "MILKSHAKE" button. 7. When the program is completed, turn the outer bowl and release it from the machine. 8. Transfer the shake into serving glasses and enjoy immediately.

Nutritional Information per Serving:

Calories: 139 |Fat: 7.2g|Sat Fat: 4.5g|Carbohydrates: 14.8g|Fiber: 0.4g|Sugar: 13.7g|Protein: 3.7g

Chocolate Brownies Milkshake

Preparation Time: 10 minutes | Servings: 2

Ingredients:

1 cup chocolate ice cream   2 tablespoons peanut butter
½ cup whole milk   1¼ cups brownies, cut up

Preparation:

1. In an empty Ninja CREAMi pint container, put in the ice cream. 2. Top with the remaining ingredients and gently blend to incorporate. 3. Arrange the container into the outer bowl of Ninja CREAMi. 4. Install the "Creamerizer Paddle" onto the lid of outer bowl. 5. Then rotate the lid clockwise to lock. 6. Press "Power" button to turn on the unit. 7. Then press "MILKSHAKE" button. 8. When the program is completed, turn the outer bowl and release it from the machine. 9. Transfer the shake into serving glasses and enjoy immediately.

Nutritional Information per Serving:

Calories: 339 |Fat: 22.3g|Sat Fat: 7.3g|Carbohydrates: 29g|Fiber: 1.2g|Sugar: 11.7g|Protein: 9g

Chai Tea Coconut Milkshake

Preparation Time: 10 minutes | Cooking Time: 5 minutes | Servings: 2

Ingredients:

½ cup coconut milk

2 chai tea bags

1½ cups vanilla coconut milk ice cream

Preparation:

1. In a small saucepan, put in coconut milk on burner at around medium heat and cook until boiling. 2. Take off from burner and add in the chai tea bags. 3. Cover the pan and let it steep until cooled thoroughly. 4. After cooling, squeeze the tea bags into the milk. 5. Then discard the tea bags. 6. In an empty Ninja CREAMi pint container, put in the ice cream. 7. With a spoon, create a 1½-inch wide hole in the center that reaches the bottom of the pint container. 8. Add the chai coconut milk into the hole. 9. Arrange the container into the outer bowl of Ninja CREAMi. 10. Install the "Creamerizer Paddle" onto the lid of outer bowl. 11. Then rotate the lid clockwise to lock. 12. Press "Power" button to turn on the unit. 13. Then press "MILKSHAKE" button. 14. When the program is completed, turn the outer bowl and release it from the machine. 15. Transfer the shake into serving glasses and enjoy immediately.

Nutritional Information per Serving:

Calories: 241 |Fat: 19.6g|Sat Fat: 16.1g|Carbohydrates: 15.3g|Fiber: 1.7g|Sugar: 12.5g|Protein: 3.1g

Tasty Chocolate Hazelnut Milkshake

Preparation Time: 10 minutes | Servings: 2

Ingredients:

1½ cups chocolate ice cream

½ cup whole milk

¼ cup hazelnut spread

Preparation:

1. In an empty Ninja CREAMi pint container, put in the ice cream. 2. Top with the remaining ingredients and gently blend to incorporate. 3. Arrange the container into the outer bowl of Ninja CREAMi. 4. Install the "Creamerizer Paddle" onto the lid of outer bowl. 5. Then rotate the lid clockwise to lock. 6. Press "Power" button to turn on the unit. 7. Then press "MILKSHAKE" button. 8. When the program is completed, turn the outer bowl and release it from the machine. 9. Transfer the shake into serving glasses and enjoy immediately.

Nutritional Information per Serving:

Calories: 329 |Fat: 19.2g|Sat Fat: 7.7g|Carbohydrates: 34.8g|Fiber: 1.4g|Sugar: 32.7g|Protein: 5.9g

Flavorful Coffee Milkshake

Preparation Time: 10 minutes | Servings: 2

Ingredients:

1½ cups coffee ice cream

½ cup milk

2 tablespoons sweetened condensed milk

¼ teaspoon salt

Preparation:

1. In an empty Ninja CREAMi pint container, put in the ice cream. 2. Top with the remaining ingredients and gently blend to incorporate. 3. Arrange the container into the outer bowl of Ninja CREAMi. 4. Install the "Creamerizer Paddle" onto the lid of outer bowl. 5. Then rotate the lid clockwise to lock. 6. Press "Power" button to turn on the unit. 7. Then press "MILKSHAKE" button. 8. When the program is completed, turn the outer bowl and release it from the machine. 9. Transfer the shake into serving glasses and enjoy immediately.

Nutritional Information per Serving:

Calories: 1954 |Fat: 8.2g|Sat Fat: 5.2g|Carbohydrates: 25.4g|Fiber: 0.4g|Sugar: 23.6g|Protein: 5.2g

Caramel Pretzels Milkshake

Preparation Time: 10 minutes | Servings: 2

Ingredients:

1¼ cups vanilla ice cream

¼ cup whole milk

2 tablespoons caramel sauce

⅓ cup pretzels, broken

1 pinch of sea salt

Preparation:

1. In an empty Ninja CREAMi pint container, put in the ice cream. 2. With a spoon, create a 1½-inch wide hole in the center that reaches the bottom of the pint container. 3. Put in remaining ingredients into the hole. 4. Arrange the container into the outer bowl of Ninja CREAMi. 5. Install the "Creamerizer Paddle" onto the lid of outer bowl. 6. Then rotate the lid clockwise to lock. 7. Press "Power" button to turn on the unit. 8. Then press "MILKSHAKE" button. 9. When the program is completed, turn the outer bowl and release it from the machine. 10. Transfer the shake into serving glasses and enjoy immediately.

Nutritional Information per Serving:

Calories: 231 |Fat: 5.9g|Sat Fat: 3.5g|Carbohydrates: 40.7g|Fiber: 1.1g|Sugar: 10.9g|Protein: 4.8g

Vanilla Apple Pie Milkshake

Preparation Time: 10 minutes | Servings: 2

Ingredients:

1½ cups vanilla ice cream

¼ cup whole milk

2 ounces premade apple pie

Preparation:

1. In an empty Ninja CREAMi pint container, put in the ice cream. 2. With a spoon, create a 1½-inch wide hole in the center that reaches the bottom of the pint container. 3. Put in remaining ingredients into the hole. 4. Arrange the container into the outer bowl of Ninja CREAMi. 5. Install the "Creamerizer Paddle" onto the lid of outer bowl. 6. Then rotate the lid clockwise to lock. 7. Press "Power" button to turn on the unit. 8. Then press "MILKSHAKE" button. 9. When the program is completed, turn the outer bowl and release it from the machine. 10. Transfer the shake into serving glasses and enjoy immediately.

Nutritional Information per Serving:

Calories: 191 |Fat: 9.6g|Sat Fat: 4.6g|Carbohydrates: 22.7g|Fiber: 0.7g|Sugar: 16.1g|Protein: 3.2g

Chapter 2 Smoothie Bowls

Strawberry & Dragon Fruit Smoothie Bowl

Preparation Time: 10 minutes | Servings: 2

Ingredients:

½ cup coconut water
2 cups frozen dragon fruit, chopped
2 cup frozen strawberries, hulled

1 banana, peeled
1-2 tablespoons honey

Preparation:

1. In a high-powered blender, put in water and remaining ingredients and process to form a smooth mixture. 2. Transfer the blended mixture into an empty Ninja CREAMi pint container. 3. Cover the container with storage lid and freeze for 24 hours. 4. After 24 hours, take off the lid from container and arrange into the outer bowl of Ninja CREAMi. 5. Install the "Creamerizer Paddle" onto the lid of outer bowl. 6. Then rotate the lid clockwise to lock. 7. Press "Power" button to turn on the unit. 8. Then press "SMOOTHIE BOWL" button. 9. When the program is completed, turn the outer bowl and release it from the machine. 10. Transfer the smoothie into serving bowls and enjoy immediately.

Nutritional Information per Serving:

Calories: 187 |Fat: 0.7g|Sat Fat: 0.2g|Carbohydrates: 47.6g|Fiber: 5.1g|Sugar: 36.5g|Protein: 2.1g

Mango Yogurt Smoothie Bowl

Preparation Time: 10 minutes | Servings: 2

Ingredients:

1 cup frozen mango chunks
1 cup plain Greek yogurt

¼ cup fresh pineapple juice
2 tablespoons honey

Preparation:

1. In a high-powered blender, put in mango and remaining ingredients and process to form a smooth mixture. 2. Transfer the blended mixture into an empty Ninja CREAMi pint container. 3. Cover the container with storage lid and freeze for 24 hours. 4. After 24 hours, take off the lid from container and arrange into the outer bowl of Ninja CREAMi. 5. Install the "Creamerizer Paddle" onto the lid of outer bowl. 6. Then rotate the lid clockwise to lock. 7. Press "Power" button to turn on the unit. 8. Then press "SMOOTHIE BOWL" button. 9. When the program is completed, turn the outer bowl and release it from the machine. 10. Transfer the smoothie into serving bowls and enjoy immediately.

Nutritional Information per Serving:

Calories: 217 |Fat: 1.9g|Sat Fat: 1.3g|Carbohydrates: 42.3g|Fiber: 1.4g|Sugar: 40.3g|Protein: 7.8g

Orange Strawberry Smoothie Bowl

Preparation Time: 10 minutes | Servings: 2

Ingredients:

1 cup frozen strawberries
1 cup strawberry yogurt
¼ cup fresh orange juice

2 tablespoons maple syrup
¼ teaspoon vanilla extract

Preparation:

1. In a high-powered blender, put in strawberries and remaining ingredients and process to form a smooth mixture. 2. Transfer the blended mixture into an empty Ninja CREAMi pint container. 3. Cover the container with storage lid and freeze for 24 hours. 4. After 24 hours, take off the lid from container and arrange into the outer bowl of Ninja CREAMi. 5. Install the "Creamerizer Paddle" onto the lid of outer bowl. 6. Then rotate the lid clockwise to lock. 7. Press "Power" button to turn on the unit. 8. Then press "SMOOTHIE BOWL" button. 9. When the program is completed, turn the outer bowl and release it from the machine. 10. Transfer the smoothie into serving bowls and enjoy immediately.

Nutritional Information per Serving:

Calories: 212 |Fat: 1.7g|Sat Fat: 0.9g|Carbohydrates: 45.1g|Fiber: 1.5g|Sugar: 40.9g|Protein: 5.6g

Blueberry Yogurt Smoothie Bowl

Preparation Time: 10 minutes | Servings: 2

Ingredients:

2 cups fresh blueberries
½ cup plain yogurt

¼ cup fresh orange juice
1 tablespoon maple syrup

Preparation:

1. In an empty Ninja CREAMi pint container, put in the blueberries and with the back of a spoon, firmly press the berries below the MAX FILL line. 2. Put in yogurt, orange juice and maple syrup and blend to incorporate. 3. Cover the container with storage lid and freeze for 24 hours. 4. After 24 hours, take off the lid from container and arrange into the outer bowl of Ninja CREAMi. 5. Install the "Creamerizer Paddle" onto the lid of outer bowl. 6. Then rotate the lid clockwise to lock. 7. Press "Power" button to turn on the unit. 8. Then press "SMOOTHIE BOWL" button. 9. When the program is completed, turn the outer bowl and release it from the machine. 10. Transfer the smoothie into serving bowls and enjoy immediately.

Nutritional Information per Serving:

Calories: 167 |Fat: 1.3g|Sat Fat: 0.6g|Carbohydrates: 35.2g|Fiber: 3.6g|Sugar: 27.3g|Protein: 4.8g

Blackberry Smoothie Bowl

Preparation Time: 10 minutes | Servings: 2

Ingredients:

1 scoop vanilla protein powder

¾ cup milk

½ cup frozen blackberries

1 medium banana, sliced into coins

Preparation:

1. In a small-sized bowl, blend together the protein powder and milk. 2. Place the blackberries and banana into an empty Ninja CREAMi pint container. 3. Top with milk mixture. 4. Cover the container with storage lid and freeze for 24 hours. 5. After 24 hours, take off the lid from container and arrange into the outer bowl of Ninja CREAMi. 6. Install the "Creamerizer Paddle" onto the lid of outer bowl. 7. Then rotate the lid clockwise to lock. 8. Press "Power" button to turn on the unit. 9. Then press "SMOOTHIE BOWL" button. 10. When the program is completed, turn the outer bowl and release it from the machine. 11. Transfer the smoothie into serving bowls and enjoy immediately.

Nutritional Information per Serving:

Calories: 167 |Fat: 2.5g|Sat Fat: 1.2g|Carbohydrates: 22.5g|Fiber: 3.4g|Sugar: 13.6g|Protein: 16.3g

Pineapple Green Smoothie

Preparation Time: 10 minutes | Servings: 4

Ingredients:

1 cup avocado, peel removed, pitted and cut up

1 cup fresh kale

¼ cup frozen pineapple chunks

¼ cup pineapple juice

¼ cup raw agave nectar

¼ cup unsweetened coconut milk

Preparation:

1. In a high-powered blender, put in avocado and remaining ingredients and process to form a smooth mixture. 2. Transfer the blended mixture into an empty Ninja CREAMi pint container. 3. Cover the container with storage lid and freeze for 24 hours. 4. After 24 hours, take off the lid from container and arrange into the outer bowl of Ninja CREAMi. 5. Install the "Creamerizer Paddle" onto the lid of outer bowl. 6. Then rotate the lid clockwise to lock. 7. Press "Power" button to turn on the unit. 8. Then press "SMOOTHIE BOWL" button. 9. When the program is completed, turn the outer bowl and release it from the machine. 10. Transfer the smoothie into serving bowls and enjoy immediately.

Nutritional Information per Serving:

Calories: 199 |Fat: 10.7g|Sat Fat: 4.7g|Carbohydrates: 27.1g|Fiber: 3.2g|Sugar: 21.5g|Protein: 1.7g

Chocolate Banana Smoothie Bowl

Preparation Time: 10 minutes | Servings: 2

Ingredients:

1 cup whole milk

2 tablespoon unsweetened cocoa powder

1 tablespoon chia seeds

1½ bananas, peeled and sliced

1½ scoops chocolate protein powder

Preparation:

1. In a high-powered blender, put in water and remaining ingredients and process to form a smooth mixture. 2. Transfer the blended mixture into an empty Ninja CREAMi pint container. 3. Cover the container with storage lid and freeze for 24 hours. 4. After 24 hours, take off the lid from container and arrange into the outer bowl of Ninja CREAMi. 5. Install the "Creamerizer Paddle" onto the lid of outer bowl. 6. Then rotate the lid clockwise to lock. 7. Press "Power" button to turn on the unit. 8. Then press "SMOOTHIE BOWL" button. 9. When the program is completed, turn the outer bowl and release it from the machine. 10. Transfer the smoothie into serving bowls and enjoy immediately.

Nutritional Information per Serving:

Calories: 267 |Fat: 7.5g|Sat Fat: 3.7g|Carbohydrates: 33.4g|Fiber: 6g|Sugar: 18.9g|Protein: 22.8g

Apple Cherry Smoothie Bowl

Preparation Time: 10 minutes | Servings: 2

Ingredients:

2 cups frozen cherries

1 cup apple juice

⅓ cup maple syrup

½ teaspoon ground cinnamon

Preparation:

1. In an empty Ninja CREAMi pint container, put in cherries. 2. In a large-sized bowl, put in the apple juice, maple syrup and cinnamon and whisk until blended thoroughly. 3. Place the blended mixture over the cherries and lightly blend to incorporate. 4. Cover the container with storage lid and freeze for 24 hours. 5. After 24 hours, take off the lid from container and arrange into the outer bowl of Ninja CREAMi. 6. Install the "Creamerizer Paddle" onto the lid of outer bowl. 7. Then rotate the lid clockwise to lock. 8. Press "Power" button to turn on the unit. 9. Then press "SMOOTHIE BOWL" button. 10. When the program is completed, turn the outer bowl and release it from the machine. 11. Transfer the smoothie into serving bowls and enjoy immediately.

Nutritional Information per Serving:

Calories: 285 |Fat: 0.3g|Sat Fat: 0.1g|Carbohydrates: 71.7g|Fiber: 3.6g|Sugar: 62.3g|Protein: 2.1g

Pineapple Coconut Milk Smoothie Bowl

Preparation Time: 10 minutes | Servings: 4

Ingredients:

2 cups pineapple, cut into 1-inch pieces

1 (14-ounces) can full-fat coconut milk

Preparation:

1. Place the pineapple pieces into an empty Ninja CREAMi pint container. 2. Top with coconut milk and blend to incorporate. 3. Cover the container with storage lid and freeze for 24 hours. 4. After 24 hours, take off the lid from container and arrange into the outer bowl of Ninja CREAMi. 5. Install the "Creamerizer Paddle" onto the lid of outer bowl. 6. Then rotate the lid clockwise to lock. 7. Press "Power" button to turn on the unit. 8. Then press "SMOOTHIE BOWL" button. 9. When the program is completed, turn the outer bowl and release it from the machine. 10. Transfer the smoothie into serving bowls and enjoy immediately.

Nutritional Information per Serving:

Calories: 224 |Fat: 18.4g|Sat Fat: 16.8g|Carbohydrates: 13.9g|Fiber: 1.2g|Sugar: 9.7g|Protein: 2g

Berry Medley Smoothie Bowl

Preparation Time: 10 minutes | Servings: 2

Ingredients:

2 cups frozen berry medley
½ cup grapefruit juice

1 tablespoon honey

Preparation:

1. In a high-powered blender, put in berry medley and remaining ingredients and process to form a smooth mixture. 2. Transfer the blended mixture into an empty Ninja CREAMi pint container. 3. Cover the container with storage lid and freeze for 24 hours. 4. After 24 hours, take off the lid from container and arrange into the outer bowl of Ninja CREAMi. 5. Install the "Creamerizer Paddle" onto the lid of outer bowl. 6. Then rotate the lid clockwise to lock. 7. Press "Power" button to turn on the unit. 8. Then press "SMOOTHIE BOWL" button. 9. When the program is completed, turn the outer bowl and release it from the machine. 10. Transfer the smoothie into serving bowls and enjoy immediately.

Nutritional Information per Serving:

Calories: 120 |Fat: 0.6g|Sat Fat: 0g|Carbohydrates: 30.3g|Fiber: 6.7g|Sugar: 22.6g|Protein: 0.4g

Strawberry & Pineapple Smoothie

Preparation Time: 10 minutes | Servings: 4

Ingredients:

2 cups frozen sliced strawberries

¾ cup pineapple juice

3 tablespoons raw agave nectar

Preparation:

1. In an empty Ninja CREAMi pint container, put in ice strawberries, followed by pineapple juice and agave. 2. Cover the container with storage lid and freeze for 24 hours. 3. After 24 hours, take off the lid from container and arrange into the outer bowl of Ninja CREAMi. 4. Install the "Creamerizer Paddle" onto the lid of outer bowl. 5. Then rotate the lid clockwise to lock. 6. Press "Power" button to turn on the unit. 7. Then press "SMOOTHIE BOWL" button. 8. When the program is completed, turn the outer bowl and release it from the machine. 9. Transfer the smoothie into serving bowls and enjoy immediately.

Nutritional Information per Serving:

Calories: 93 |Fat: 0.3g|Sat Fat: 0g|Carbohydrates: 23.6g|Fiber: 1.5g|Sugar: 202g|Protein: 0.7g

Peach Banana Smoothie Bowl

Preparation Time: 10 minutes | Servings: 2

Ingredients:

1 cup frozen peach chunks

1 fresh banana, peeled and halved

½ teaspoon vanilla extract

2 tablespoons whole milk

Preparation:

1. In a high-powered blender, put in peach chunks and remaining ingredients and process to form a smooth mixture. 2. Transfer the blended mixture into an empty Ninja CREAMi pint container. 3. Cover the container with storage lid and freeze for 24 hours. 4. After 24 hours, take off the lid from container and arrange into the outer bowl of Ninja CREAMi. 5. Install the "Creamerizer Paddle" onto the lid of outer bowl. 6. Then rotate the lid clockwise to lock. 7. Press "Power" button to turn on the unit. 8. Then press "SMOOTHIE BOWL" button. 9. When the program is completed, turn the outer bowl and release it from the machine. 10. Transfer the smoothie into serving bowls and enjoy immediately.

Nutritional Information per Serving:

Calories: 94 |Fat: 0.9g|Sat Fat: 0.4g|Carbohydrates: 21.3g|Fiber: 2.7g|Sugar: 15.1g|Protein: 1.8g

Honey Raspberry Smoothie Bowl

Preparation Time: 10 minutes | Servings: 4

Ingredients:

2 tablespoons vanilla protein powder
¼ cup honey
¼ cup orange juice
½ cup coconut milk

1 cup banana, peel removed and cut in ½-inch pieces
1 cup fresh raspberries

Preparation:

1. In a large-sized bowl, put in protein powder, honey, apple juice and coconut milk and whisk to incorporate thoroughly. 2. Place the banana and raspberries into an empty Ninja CREAMi pint container and with the back of a spoon, firmly press the fruit below the MAX FILL line. 3. Top with milk mixture and blend to incorporate thoroughly. 4. Cover the container with storage lid and freeze for 24 hours. 5. After 24 hours, take off the lid from container and arrange into the outer bowl of Ninja CREAMi. 6. Install the "Creamerizer Paddle" onto the lid of outer bowl. 7. Then rotate the lid clockwise to lock. 8. Press "Power" button to turn on the unit. 9. Then press "SMOOTHIE BOWL" button. 10. When the program is completed, turn the outer bowl and release it from the machine. 11. Transfer the smoothie into serving bowls and enjoy immediately.

Nutritional Information per Serving:

Calories: 288 |Fat: 16.2g|Sat Fat: 13.8g|Carbohydrates: 32g|Fiber: 7.6g|Sugar: 16.8g|Protein: 9.2g

Refreshing Pineapple Smoothie Bowl

Preparation Time: 10 minutes | Servings: 2

Ingredients:

2 cups fresh pineapple pieces
14 ounces coconut milk

2 tablespoons maple syrup
¼ teaspoon vanilla extract

Preparation:

1. Place the pineapple pieces into an empty Ninja CREAMi pint container. 2. Top with coconut milk, maple syrup and vanilla extract and blend to incorporate. 3. Cover the container with the storage lid and freeze for 24 hours. 4. After 24 hours, take off the lid from container and arrange into the outer bowl of Ninja CREAMi. 5. Install the "Creamerizer Paddle" onto the lid of outer bowl. 6. Then rotate the lid clockwise to lock. 7. Press "Power" button to turn on the unit. 8. Then press "SMOOTHIE BOWL" button. 9. When the program is completed, turn the outer bowl and release it from the machine. 10. Transfer the smoothie into serving bowls and enjoy immediately.

Nutritional Information per Serving:

Calories: 433 |Fat: 27.5g|Sat Fat: 24.8g|Carbohydrates: 40.1g|Fiber: 2.3g|Sugar: 33.2g|Protein: 3.4g

Fresh Blueberry Smoothie Bowl

Preparation Time: 10 minutes | Servings: 4

Ingredients:

2 tablespoons protein powder
¼ cup maple syrup
¼ cup apple juice
½ cup milk

1 cup banana, peel removed and cut in ½-inch
pieces
1 cup fresh blueberries

Preparation:

1. In a large-sized bowl, put in protein powder, maple syrup, apple juice and milk and whisk to incorporate thoroughly. 2. Place the banana and blueberries into an empty Ninja CREAMi pint container and with the back of a spoon, firmly press the fruit below the MAX FILL line. 3. Top with milk mixture and blend to incorporate thoroughly. 4. Cover the container with storage lid and freeze for 24 hours. 5. After 24 hours, take off the lid from container and arrange into the outer bowl of Ninja CREAMi. 6. Install the "Creamerizer Paddle" onto the lid of outer bowl. 7. Then rotate the lid clockwise to lock. 8. Press "Power" button to turn on the unit. 9. Then press "SMOOTHIE BOWL" button. 10. When the program is completed, turn the outer bowl and release it from the machine. 11. Transfer the smoothie into serving bowls and enjoy immediately.

Nutritional Information per Serving:

Calories: 142 |Fat: 1.2g|Sat Fat: 0.6g|Carbohydrates: 30.7g|Fiber: 1.9g|Sugar: 22.9g|Protein: 4.4g

Strawberry Yogurt Smoothie Bowl

Preparation Time: 10 minutes | Servings: 4

Ingredients:

3 cups fresh strawberries, quartered
¼ cup strawberry yogurt

1 tablespoon maple syrup

Preparation:

1. In a high-powered blender, put in strawberries and remaining ingredients and process to form a smooth mixture. 2. Transfer the blended mixture into an empty Ninja CREAMi pint container. 3. Cover the container with storage lid and freeze for 24 hours. 4. After 24 hours, take off the lid from container and arrange into the outer bowl of Ninja CREAMi. 5. Install the "Creamerizer Paddle" onto the lid of outer bowl. 6. Then rotate the lid clockwise to lock. 7. Press "Power" button to turn on the unit. 8. Then press "SMOOTHIE BOWL" button. 9. When the program is completed, turn the outer bowl and release it from the machine. 10. Transfer the smoothie into serving bowls and enjoy immediately.

Nutritional Information per Serving:

Calories: 95 |Fat: 2.1g|Sat Fat: 0g|Carbohydrates: 17.3g|Fiber: 2.2g|Sugar: 8.3g|Protein: 3g

Raspberry Orange Smoothie Bowl

Preparation Time: 10 minutes | Servings: 2

Ingredients:

2 cups frozen raspberries
½ cup orange juice

1 tablespoon maple syrup

Preparation:

1. In a high-powered blender, put in raspberries and remaining ingredients and process to form a smooth mixture. 2. Transfer the blended mixture into an empty Ninja CREAMi pint container. 3. Cover the container with storage lid and freeze for 24 hours. 4. After 24 hours, take off the lid from container and arrange into the outer bowl of Ninja CREAMi. 5. Install the "Creamerizer Paddle" onto the lid of outer bowl. 6. Then rotate the lid clockwise to lock. 7. Press "Power" button to turn on the unit. 8. Then press "SMOOTHIE BOWL" button. 9. When the program is completed, turn the outer bowl and release it from the machine. 10. Transfer the smoothie into serving bowls and enjoy immediately.

Nutritional Information per Serving:

Calories: 118 |Fat: 1g|Sat Fat: 0g|Carbohydrates: 27.9g|Fiber: 8.1g|Sugar: 16.6g|Protein: 1.9g

Tofu and Papaya Smoothie Bowl

Preparation Time: 10 minutes | Servings: 4

Ingredients:

½ cup whole milk
¼ cup fresh orange juice
2 tablespoons vanilla protein powder
4-5 tablespoons honey

¼ teaspoon vanilla extract
1 cup tofu, pressed, drained and cut in ½-inch pieces
1 cup papaya, peeled and cut in ½-inch pieces

Preparation:

1. In a large-sized bowl, put in the milk, orange juice, protein powder, honey and vanilla extract and whisk until blended thoroughly. 2. Place the tofu and papaya into an empty Ninja CREAMi pint container and with the back of a spoon, firmly press them below the MAX FILL line. 3. Top with milk mixture and blend to incorporate thoroughly. 4. Cover the container with storage lid and freeze for 24 hours. 5. After 24 hours, take off the lid from container and arrange into the outer bowl of Ninja CREAMi. 6. Install the "Creamerizer Paddle" onto the lid of outer bowl. 7. Then rotate the lid clockwise to lock. 8. Press "Power" button to turn on the unit. 9. Then press "SMOOTHIE BOWL" button. 10. When the program is completed, turn the outer bowl and release it from the machine. 11. Transfer the smoothie into serving bowls and enjoy immediately.

Nutritional Information per Serving:

Calories: 325 |Fat: 7.6g|Sat Fat: 2.3g|Carbohydrates: 51.2g|Fiber: 2.5g|Sugar: 47g|Protein: 19.1g

Peach Coffee Smoothie Bowl

Preparation Time: 10 minutes | Servings: 4

Ingredients:

1 cup brewed coffee

½ cup coconut milk

2 tablespoons mocha almond butter

1 cup peach, peel removed, pitted and cut up

1 large banana, peel removed and sliced

Preparation:

1. In a high-powered blender, put in peach and remaining ingredients and process to form a smooth mixture. 2. Transfer the blended mixture into an empty Ninja CREAMi pint container. 3. Cover the container with storage lid and freeze for 24 hours. 4. After 24 hours, take off the lid from container and arrange into the outer bowl of Ninja CREAMi. 5. Install the "Creamerizer Paddle" onto the lid of outer bowl. 6. Then rotate the lid clockwise to lock. 7. Press "Power" button to turn on the unit. 8. Then press "SMOOTHIE BOWL" button. 9. When the program is completed, turn the outer bowl and release it from the machine. 10. Transfer the smoothie into serving bowls and enjoy immediately.

Nutritional Information per Serving:

Calories: 164 |Fat: 11.9g|Sat Fat: 6.7g|Carbohydrates: 14.4g|Fiber: 2.9g|Sugar: 9g|Protein: 3.2g

Delicious Dragon Fruit& Mango Smoothie Bowl

Preparation Time: 10 minutes | Servings: 4

Ingredients:

1 frozen banana, cut up

1 cup frozen mango chunks

2 cups frozen dragon fruit, cut up

¼ cup full-fat coconut milk

Preparation:

1. In a high-powered blender, put in frozen dragon fruit and remaining ingredients and process to form a smooth mixture. 2. Transfer the blended mixture into an empty Ninja CREAMi pint container. 3. Cover the container with storage lid and freeze for 24 hours. 4. After 24 hours, take off the lid from container and arrange into the outer bowl of Ninja CREAMi. 5. Install the "Creamerizer Paddle" onto the lid of outer bowl. 6. Then rotate the lid clockwise to lock. 7. Press "Power" button to turn on the unit. 8. Then press "SMOOTHIE BOWL" button. 9. When the program is completed, turn the outer bowl and release it from the machine. 10. Transfer the smoothie into serving bowls and enjoy immediately.

Nutritional Information per Serving:

Calories: 104 |Fat: 3.3g|Sat Fat: 2.8g|Carbohydrates: 19.4g|Fiber: 1.4g|Sugar: 15.5g|Protein: 0.9g

Mixed Fruit Smoothie

Preparation Time: 10 minutes | Servings: 4

Ingredients:

2 cups frozen mixed fruit

¼ cup frozen sliced strawberries

¼ cup pineapple orange Juice

¼ cup raw agave nectar

¼ cup unsweetened coconut milk

Preparation:

1. In a high-powered blender, put in mixed fruit and remaining ingredients and process to form a smooth mixture. 2. Transfer the blended mixture into an empty Ninja CREAMi pint container. 3. Cover the container with storage lid and freeze for 24 hours. 4. After 24 hours, take off the lid from container and arrange into the outer bowl of Ninja CREAMi. 5. Install the "Creamerizer Paddle" onto the lid of outer bowl. 6. Then rotate the lid clockwise to lock. 7. Press "Power" button to turn on the unit. 8. Then press "SMOOTHIE BOWL" button. 9. When the program is completed, turn the outer bowl and release it from the machine. 10. Transfer the smoothie into serving bowls and enjoy immediately.

Nutritional Information per Serving:

Calories: 134 |Fat: 3.6g|Sat Fat: 0g|Carbohydrates: 27.1g|Fiber: 2g|Sugar: 24.2g|Protein: 0.5g

Cottage Cheese Chocolate Ice Cream

Preparation Time: 10 minutes | Servings: 4

Ingredients:

1 cup cottage cheese

1 cup chocolate milk

2 tablespoons honey

1 scoop chocolate protein powder

½ teaspoon vanilla extract

1 teaspoon ground cinnamon

Pinch of salt

Preparation:

1. In a high-powered blender, put in cottage cheese and remaining ingredients and process to form a smooth mixture. 2. Transfer the blended mixture into an empty Ninja CREAMi pint container. 3. Cover the container with storage lid and freeze for 24 hours. 4. After 24 hours, take off the lid from container and arrange into the outer bowl of Ninja CREAMi. 5. Install the "Creamerizer Paddle" onto the lid of outer bowl. 6. Then rotate the lid clockwise to lock. 7. Press "Power" button to turn on the unit. 8. Then press "ICE CREAM" button. 9. When the program is completed, turn the outer bowl and release it from the machine. 10. Transfer the ice cream into serving bowls and enjoy immediately.

Nutritional Information per Serving:

Calories: 167 |Fat: 3.6g|Sat Fat: 2.3g|Carbohydrates: 18.8g|Fiber: 1g|Sugar: 15.4g|Protein: 15.2g

Simple Banana Ice Cream

Preparation Time: 10 minutes | Servings: 4

Ingredients:

2 large ripe bananas, peeled and cut into small chunks

½ cup whole milk

½ cup heavy cream

3-4 drops liquid stevia

¾ teaspoon vanilla extract

Preparation:

1. In a large-sized high-powered blender, put in bananas and remaining ingredients and process to form a smooth mixture. 2. Transfer the blended mixture into an empty Ninja CREAMi pint container. 3. Cover the container with storage lid and freeze for 24 hours. 4. After 24 hours, take off the lid from container and arrange into the outer bowl of Ninja CREAMi. 5. Install the "Creamerizer Paddle" onto the lid of outer bowl. 6. Then rotate the lid clockwise to lock. 7. Press "Power" button to turn on the unit. 8. Then press "ICE CREAM" button. 9. When the program is completed, turn the outer bowl and release it from the machine. 10. Transfer the ice cream into serving bowls and enjoy immediately.

Nutritional Information per Serving:

Calories: 125 |Fat: 6.7g|Sat Fat: 4.1g|Carbohydrates: 15.4g|Fiber: 1.5g|Sugar: 8.9g|Protein: 1.9g

Pumpkin Honey Ice Cream

Preparation Time: 10 minutes | Servings: 4

Ingredients:

1¼ cups whole milk
1 teaspoon vanilla extract
½ cup pumpkin puree

1½ teaspoons pumpkin pie spice
¼ cup honey

Preparation:

1. In a bowl, put in milk and remaining ingredients and whisk until blended thoroughly. 2. Transfer the blended mixture into an empty Ninja CREAMi pint container. 3. Cover the container with storage lid and freeze for 24 hours. 4. After 24 hours, take off the lid from container and arrange into the outer bowl of Ninja CREAMi. 5. Install the "Creamerizer Paddle" onto the lid of outer bowl. 6. Then rotate the lid clockwise to lock. 7. Press "Power" button to turn on the unit. 8. Then press "ICE CREAM" button. 9. When the program is completed, turn the outer bowl and release it from the machine. 10. Transfer the ice cream into serving bowls and enjoy immediately.

Nutritional Information per Serving:

Calories: 181 |Fat: 5.6g|Sat Fat: 3.2g|Carbohydrates: 28.1g|Fiber: 1g|Sugar: 27.4g|Protein: 5.8g

Fresh Strawberry Ice Cream

Preparation Time: 10 minutes | Servings: 4

Ingredients:

1 cup heavy cream
1½ cups fresh strawberries, sliced

3 tablespoons sugar
1 teaspoon vanilla extract

Preparation:

1. In a bowl, put in the heavy cream and whisk until smooth. 2. Put in strawberry slices and with the back of a fork, lightly mash them. 3. Add in the sugar and vanilla extract and blend to incorporate thoroughly. 4. Transfer the blended mixture into an empty Ninja CREAMi pint container. 5. Cover the container with storage lid and freeze for 24 hours. 6. After 24 hours, take off the lid from container and arrange into the outer bowl of Ninja CREAMi. 7. Install the "Creamerizer Paddle" onto the lid of outer bowl. 8. Then rotate the lid clockwise to lock. 9. Press "Power" button to turn on the unit. 10. Then press "ICE CREAM" button. 11. When the program is completed, turn the outer bowl and release it from the machine. 12. Transfer the ice cream into serving bowls and enjoy immediately.

Nutritional Information per Serving:

Calories: 158 |Fat: 11.3g|Sat Fat: 6.9g|Carbohydrates: 14.1g|Fiber: 1.1g|Sugar: 11.8g|Protein: 1g

Flavorful Blueberry Ice Cream

Preparation Time: 10 minutes | Servings: 4

Ingredients:

1 cup whole milk

1¼ cups frozen blueberries

1 teaspoon vanilla extract

Preparation:

1. In a high-powered blender, put in milk and remaining ingredients and process to form a smooth mixture. 2. Transfer the blended mixture into an empty Ninja CREAMi pint container. 3. Cover the container with storage lid and freeze for 24 hours. 4. After 24 hours, take off the lid from container and arrange into the outer bowl of Ninja CREAMi. 5. Install the "Creamerizer Paddle" onto the lid of outer bowl. 6. Then rotate the lid clockwise to lock. 7. Press "Power" button to turn on the unit. 8. Then press "ICE CREAM" button. 9. When the program is completed, turn the outer bowl and release it from the machine. 10. Transfer the ice cream into serving bowls and enjoy immediately.

Nutritional Information per Serving:

Calories: 66 |Fat: 2.1g|Sat Fat: 1.1g|Carbohydrates: 9.5g|Fiber: 1.1g|Sugar: 7.8g|Protein: 2.3g

Sweet Blackberry Ice Cream

Preparation Time: 10 minutes | Servings: 4

Ingredients:

1 cup fresh blackberries

¼ cup granulated sugar

1 cup whole milk

½ cup heavy whipping cream

Preparation:

1. In a small-sized saucepan, put in blackberries and sugar and blend to incorporate. 2. Place the pan of blackberries on burner at around medium heat and cook for approximately 3-5 minutes, stirring occasionally. 3. Take off the pan of blackberries from burner and transfer in to a small-sized bowl. 4. Set aside to cool for a few minutes. 5. In the bowl of blackberries, put in milk and heavy whipping cream and with an immersion blender, blend until smooth. 6. Transfer the blended mixture into an empty Ninja CREAMi pint container. 7. Cover the container with storage lid and freeze for 24 hours. 8. After 24 hours, take off the lid from container and arrange into the outer bowl of Ninja CREAMi. 9. Install the "Creamerizer Paddle" onto the lid of outer bowl. 10. Then rotate the lid clockwise to lock. 11. Press "Power" button to turn on the unit. 12. Then press "ICE CREAM" button. 13. When the program is completed, turn the outer bowl and release it from the machine. 14. Transfer the ice cream into serving bowls and enjoy immediately.

Nutritional Information per Serving:

Calories: 151 |Fat: 7.7g|Sat Fat: 4.6g|Carbohydrates: 19.1g|Fiber: 1.9g|Sugar: 17.5g|Protein: 2.8g

Cheese Banana Pudding Ice Cream

Preparation Time: 10 minutes | Servings: 4

Ingredients:

1 cup cottage cheese
½ cup milk
4 tablespoons instant banana pudding mix

2 tablespoons heavy cream
1 tablespoon maple syrup
½ teaspoon banana extract

Preparation:

1. Place cottage cheese and remaining ingredients into a large-sized bowl and with an immersion blender, blend to incorporate. 2. Transfer the blended mixture into an empty Ninja CREAMi pint container. 3. Cover the container with storage lid and freeze for 24 hours. 4. After 24 hours, take off the lid from container and arrange into the outer bowl of Ninja CREAMi. 5. Install the "Creamerizer Paddle" onto the lid of outer bowl. 6. Then rotate the lid clockwise to lock. 7. Press "Power" button to turn on the unit. 8. Then press "ICE CREAM" button. 9. When the program is completed, turn the outer bowl and release it from the machine. 10. Transfer the ice cream into serving bowls and enjoy immediately.

Nutritional Information per Serving:

Calories: 212 |Fat: 6.2g|Sat Fat: 3.8g|Carbohydrates: 26.9g|Fiber: 0g|Sugar: 4.6g|Protein: 11.7g

Delicious Sweet Potato Ice Cream

Preparation Time: 15 minutes | Cooking Time: 10 seconds | Servings: 4

Ingredients:

1 tablespoon cream cheese
5 tablespoons white sugar
½ tablespoon corn syrup
1 teaspoon ground cinnamon

1 teaspoon vanilla extract
1 cup whole milk
¾ cup heavy cream
3 tablespoons sweet potato puree

Preparation:

1. In a large-sized microwave-safe bowl, put in the cream cheese and microwave on High for about 10 seconds. 2. Take off from the microwave and blend until smooth. 3. Put in sugar, corn syrup, cinnamon and vanilla extract and with a wire whisk, beat until the mixture looks like frosting. 4. Slowly put in milk, heavy cream and sweet potato puree and whisk until blended thoroughly. 5. Transfer the blended mixture into an empty Ninja CREAMi pint container. 6. Cover the container with storage lid and freeze for 24 hours. 7. After 24 hours, take off the lid from container and arrange into the outer bowl of Ninja CREAMi. 8. Install the "Creamerizer Paddle" onto the lid of outer bowl. 9. Then rotate the lid clockwise to lock. 10. Press "Power" button to turn on the unit. 11. Then press "ICE CREAM" button. 12. When the program is completed, turn the outer bowl and release it from the machine. 13. Transfer the ice cream into serving bowls and enjoy immediately.

Nutritional Information per Serving:

Calories: 202 |Fat: 11.2g|Sat Fat: 6.9g|Carbohydrates: 23.6g|Fiber: 0.5g|Sugar: 19.7g|Protein: 2.9g

Lemon Butterscotch Pudding Ice Cream

Preparation Time: 10 minutes | Servings: 4

Ingredients:

¾ cup coconut milk

½ cup coconut cream

¼ cup frozen lemon juice concentrate

3½ tablespoons instant butterscotch pudding mix

2 tablespoons sugar

1 teaspoon vanilla extract

Preparation:

1. In a large-sized bowl, put in oat milk and remaining ingredients and whisk until blended thoroughly. 2. Transfer the blended mixture into an empty Ninja CREAMi pint container. 3. Cover the container with storage lid and freeze for 24 hours. 4. After 24 hours, take off the lid from container and arrange into the outer bowl of Ninja CREAMi. 5. Install the "Creamerizer Paddle" onto the lid of outer bowl. 6. Then rotate the lid clockwise to lock. 7. Press "Power" button to turn on the unit. 8. Then press "ICE CREAM" button. 9. When the program is completed, turn the outer bowl and release it from the machine. 10. Transfer the ice cream into serving bowls and enjoy immediately.

Nutritional Information per Serving:

Calories: 353 |Fat: 30.8g|Sat Fat: 25.8g|Carbohydrates: 19.2g|Fiber: 1.4g|Sugar: 8.9g|Protein: 3.2g

Refreshing Orange Ice Cream

Preparation Time: 10 minutes | Servings: 4

Ingredients:

1 cup heavy cream

½ cup orange juice

⅓ cup light brown sugar

2 tablespoons cream cheese frosting

1 teaspoon vanilla extract

Preparation:

1. In a bowl, put in heavy cream and remaining ingredients and whisk to incorporate thoroughly. 2. Transfer the blended mixture into an empty Ninja CREAMi pint container. 3. Cover the container with storage lid and freeze for 24 hours. 4. After 24 hours, take off the lid from container and arrange into the outer bowl of Ninja CREAMi. 5. Install the "Creamerizer Paddle" onto the lid of outer bowl. 6. Then rotate the lid clockwise to lock. 7. Press "Power" button to turn on the unit. 8. Then press "ICE CREAM" button. 9. When the program is completed, turn the outer bowl and release it from the machine. 10. Transfer the ice cream into serving bowls and enjoy immediately.

Nutritional Information per Serving:

Calories: 191 |Fat: 12.4g|Sat Fat: 7.3g|Carbohydrates: 19.8g|Fiber: 0.1g|Sugar: 17.7g|Protein: 0.8g

Coconut Ice Cream

Preparation Time: 15 minutes | Servings: 4

Ingredients:

1 (14-ounce) can full-fat coconut milk

½ cup granulated sugar

1 teaspoon vanilla extract

Preparation:

1. In a medium-sized bowl, put in coconut milk, sugar and vanilla extract and whisk to form smooth milk. 2. Transfer the blended mixture into an empty Ninja CREAMi pint container. 3. Cover the container with the storage lid and freeze for 24 hours. 4. After 24 hours, take off the lid from container and arrange into the outer bowl of Ninja CREAMi. 5. Install the "Creamerizer Paddle" onto the lid of outer bowl. 6. Then rotate the lid clockwise to lock. 7. Press "Power" button to turn on the unit. 8. Then press "ICE CREAM" button. 9. When the program is completed, turn the outer bowl and release it from the machine. 10. Transfer the ice cream into serving bowls and enjoy immediately.

Nutritional Information per Serving:

Calories: 280 |Fat: 18.3g|Sat Fat: 16.8g|Carbohydrates: 28.2g|Fiber: 0g|Sugar: 26.7g|Protein: 1.5g

Chocolate & Cottage Cheese Ice Cream

Preparation Time: 10 minutes | Servings: 2

Ingredients:

1 cup cottage cheese

½ cup milk

2 tablespoons chocolate instant pudding mix

2 tablespoons cocoa powder

2 tablespoons heavy cream

1 tablespoon honey

½ teaspoon vanilla extract

Preparation:

1. Place cottage cheese and remaining ingredients into a large-sized bowl and with an immersion blender, blend to incorporate. 2. Transfer the blended mixture into an empty Ninja CREAMi pint container. 3. Cover the container with storage lid and freeze for 24 hours. 4. After 24 hours, take off the lid from container and arrange into the outer bowl of Ninja CREAMi. 5. Install the "Creamerizer Paddle" onto the lid of outer bowl. 6. Then rotate the lid clockwise to lock. 7. Press "Power" button to turn on the unit. 8. Then press "ICE CREAM" button. 9. When the program is completed, turn the outer bowl and release it from the machine. 10. Transfer the ice cream into serving bowls and enjoy immediately.

Nutritional Information per Serving:

Calories: 336 |Fat: 11.6g|Sat Fat: 7.1g|Carbohydrates: 38.2g|Fiber: 2g|Sugar: 23.3g|Protein: 22g

Lemon Curd Ice Cream

Preparation Time: 10 minutes | Servings: 4

Ingredients:

¼ cup lemon curd

2 tablespoons granulated sugar

2 tablespoons limoncello

1 cup heavy cream

¾ cup whole milk

1 teaspoon lemon zest, grated

Preparation:

1. In a large-sized bowl, put in lemon curd, sugar and limoncello and whisk to incorporate thoroughly. 2. Put in heavy cream, milk, and lemon zest and whisk to incorporate thoroughly. 3. Transfer the blended mixture into an empty Ninja CREAMi pint container. 4. Cover the container with storage lid and freeze for 24 hours. 5. After 24 hours, take off the lid from container and arrange into the outer bowl of Ninja CREAMi. 6. Install the "Creamerizer Paddle" onto the lid of outer bowl. 7. Then rotate the lid clockwise to lock. 8. Press "Power" button to turn on the unit. 9. Then press "ICE CREAM" button. 10. When the program is completed, turn the outer bowl and release it from the machine. 11. Transfer the ice cream into serving bowls and enjoy immediately.

Nutritional Information per Serving:

Calories: 344 |Fat: 18.6g|Sat Fat: 10.8g|Carbohydrates: 13g|Fiber: 0g|Sugar: 12.5g|Protein: 3.1g

Traditional Vanilla Ice Cream

Preparation Time: 10 minutes | Servings: 4

Ingredients:

1 cup milk

½ cup heavy cream

⅓ cup sugar

1 teaspoon vanilla extract

Preparation:

1. In a high-powered blender, put in milk and remaining ingredients and process to form a smooth mixture. 2. Transfer the blended mixture into an empty Ninja CREAMi pint container. 3. Cover the container with storage lid and freeze for 24 hours. 4. After 24 hours, take off the lid from container and arrange into the outer bowl of Ninja CREAMi. 5. Install the "Creamerizer Paddle" onto the lid of outer bowl. 6. Then rotate the lid clockwise to lock. 7. Press "Power" button to turn on the unit. 8. Then press "ICE CREAM" button. 9. When the program is completed, turn the outer bowl and release it from the machine. 10. Transfer the ice cream into serving bowls and enjoy immediately.

Nutritional Information per Serving:

Calories: 148 |Fat: 6.8g|Sat Fat: 4.2g|Carbohydrates: 20.2g|Fiber: 0g|Sugar: 19.6g|Protein: 2.3g

Chocolate Protein Ice Cream

Preparation Time: 10 minutes | Servings: 4

Ingredients:

1 (11.5 ounce) bottle chocolate protein shake

¼ cup almond milk

2 tablespoons instant chocolate pudding mix

1 tablespoon dark cocoa powder

Preparation:

1. In a large-sized bowl, put in protein shake and remaining ingredients and blend to incorporate. 2. Transfer the blended mixture into an empty Ninja CREAMi pint container. 3. Cover the container with storage lid and freeze for 24 hours. 4. After 24 hours, take off the lid from container and arrange into the outer bowl of Ninja CREAMi. 5. Install the "Creamerizer Paddle" onto the lid of outer bowl. 6. Then rotate the lid clockwise to lock. 7. Press "Power" button to turn on the unit. 8. Then press "LITE ICE CREAM" button. 9. When the program is completed, turn the outer bowl and release it from the machine. 10. Transfer the ice cream into serving bowls and enjoy immediately.

Nutritional Information per Serving:

Calories: 393 |Fat: 7.1g|Sat Fat: 3.8g|Carbohydrates: 50.6g|Fiber: 0.9g|Sugar: 36.4g|Protein: 34.8g

Refreshing Green Tea Ice Cream

Preparation Time: 10 minutes | Cooking Time: 5 minutes | Servings: 4

Ingredients:

1 cup cashew milk

3 green tea bags

1 cup coconut milk

½ cup sugar

2 tablespoons cream cheese

¼ teaspoon salt

Preparation:

1. In a medium-sized saucepan, put in cashew milk on burner at around medium heat and cook until simmering. 2. Take off saucepan from burner and add in tea bags. 3. Cover the pan and let it steep until cooled thoroughly. 4. After cooling, squeeze the tea bags into the milk. 5. Then discard the tea bags. 6. In a high-powered blender, put in green tea milk, coconut milk, sugar, cream cheese and salt and remaining ingredients and process to form a smooth mixture. 7. Transfer the blended mixture into an empty Ninja CREAMi pint container. 8. Cover the container with storage lid and freeze for 24 hours. 9. After 24 hours, take off the lid from container and arrange into the outer bowl of Ninja CREAMi. 10. Install the "Creamerizer Paddle" onto the lid of outer bowl. 11. Then rotate the lid clockwise to lock. 12. Press "Power" button to turn on the unit. 13. Then press "ICE CREAM" button. 14. When the program is completed, turn the outer bowl and release it from the machine. 15. Transfer the ice cream into serving bowls and enjoy immediately.

Nutritional Information per Serving:

Calories: 255 |Fat: 16.5g|Sat Fat: 13.8g|Carbohydrates: 28.7g|Fiber: 1.3g|Sugar: 27g|Protein: 1.8g

Homemade Lavender Ice Cream

Preparation Time: 15 minutes | Cooking Time: 25 minutes | Servings: 4

Ingredients:

1 cup whole milk

1 cup heavy cream

2 tablespoons dried lavender

2 tablespoons honey

⅓ cup monk fruit sweetener

⅛ teaspoon salt

Preparation:

1. In a medium saucepan, put in milk and heavy cream on burner at around medium heat and cook until heated through. 2. Put in lavender and cook for around 20 minutes. 3. Take off saucepan from burner and through a fine-mesh strainer, strain the mixture into a medium-sized bowl. 4. Put in honey, monk fruit sweetener and salt to bowl and whisk to incorporate thoroughly. 5. Transfer the mixture into an empty Ninja CREAMi pint container and place into an ice bath to cool. 6. After cooling, cover the container with storage lid and freeze for 24 hours. 7. After 24 hours, take off the lid from container and arrange into the outer bowl of Ninja CREAMi. 8. Install the "Creamerizer Paddle" onto the lid of outer bowl. 9. Then rotate the lid clockwise to lock. 10. Press "Power" button to turn on the unit. 11. Then press "ICE CREAM" button. 12. When the program is completed, turn the outer bowl and release it from the machine. 13. Transfer the ice cream into serving bowls and enjoy immediately.

Nutritional Information per Serving:

Calories: 140 |Fat: 13.1g|Sat Fat: 8.1g|Carbohydrates: 3.6g|Fiber: 0g|Sugar: 3.2g|Protein: 2.6g

Peppermint Coconut Ice Cream

Preparation Time: 10 minutes | Cooking Time: 15 minutes | Servings: 4

Ingredients:

¾ cup peppermint candies, crushed

1 cup unsweetened coconut milk

1 (5.4-ounce) can coconut cream

Preparation:

1. Place peppermint candies and remaining ingredients in a small-sized saucepan over medium-high heat and whisk to incorporate thoroughly. 2. Cook for around 10 minutes. 3. Transfer the mixture into an empty Ninja CREAMi pint container and place into an ice bath to cool. 4. After cooling, cover the container with storage lid and freeze for 24 hours. 5. After 24 hours, take off the lid from container and arrange into the outer bowl of Ninja CREAMi. 6. Install the "Creamerizer Paddle" onto the lid of outer bowl. 7. Then rotate the lid clockwise to lock. 8. Press "Power" button to turn on the unit. 9. Then press "ICE CREAM" button. 10. When the program is completed, turn the outer bowl and release it from the machine. 11. Transfer the ice cream into serving bowls and enjoy immediately.

Nutritional Information per Serving:

Calories: 337 |Fat: 23.6g|Sat Fat: 20.8g|Carbohydrates: 33.1g|Fiber: 2.2g|Sugar: 21.1g|Protein: 2.3g

Strawberry Coconut Milk Ice Cream

Preparation Time: 10 minutes | Servings: 4

Ingredients:

1 (13¼-ounce) can full-fat coconut milk

⅓ cup strawberry jam

1 teaspoon vanilla extract

Preparation:

1. Place coconut milk and remaining ingredients in a medium bowl and whisk to incorporate thoroughly. 2. Transfer the blended mixture into an empty Ninja CREAMi pint container. 3. Cover the container with storage lid and freeze for 24 hours. 4. After 24 hours, take off the lid from container and arrange into the outer bowl of Ninja CREAMi. 5. Install the "Creamerizer Paddle" onto the lid of outer bowl. 6. Then rotate the lid clockwise to lock. 7. Press "Power" button to turn on the unit. 8. Then press "ICE CREAM" button. 9. When the program is completed, turn the outer bowl and release it from the machine. 10. Transfer the ice cream into serving bowls and enjoy immediately.

Nutritional Information per Serving:

Calories: 281 |Fat: 17.7g|Sat Fat: 16.2g|Carbohydrates: 27.9g|Fiber: 0g|Sugar: 21.6g|Protein: 1.5g

Tasty Coffee Ice Cream

Preparation Time: 15 minutes | Cooking Time: 5 minutes | Servings: 4

Ingredients:

1 cup whole milk

2 tablespoons finely ground coffee

1 cup cream

1 tablespoon coffee liqueur

2 tablespoons agave nectar

⅓ cup monk fruit sweetener

1 teaspoon vanilla extract

Preparation:

1. In a medium-sized saucepan, put in milk on burner at around medium heat and cook until boiling. 2. Take off the saucepan of milk from burner and blend in coffee. 3. Let it steep for around 1 minute. 4. Put in cream, coffee liqueur, agave nectar, monk fruit sweetener and vanilla extract and whisk to incorporate thoroughly. 5. Transfer the mixture into an empty Ninja CREAMi pint container and place into an ice bath to cool. 6. After cooling, cover the container with storage lid and freeze for 24 hours. 7. After 24 hours, take off the lid from container and arrange into the outer bowl of Ninja CREAMi. 8. Install the "Creamerizer Paddle" onto the lid of outer bowl. 9. Then rotate the lid clockwise to lock. 10. Press "Power" button to turn on the unit. 11. Then press "ICE CREAM" button. 12. When the program is completed, turn the outer bowl and release it from the machine. 13. Transfer the ice cream into serving bowls and enjoy immediately.

Nutritional Information per Serving:

Calories: 122 |Fat: 5.3g|Sat Fat: 3.2g|Carbohydrates: 14.8g|Fiber: 0.5g|Sugar: 14.1g|Protein: 2.5g

Caramel Chocolate Ice Cream

Preparation Time: 10 minutes | Servings: 4

Ingredients:

1 (11.5 ounce) bottle caramel protein shake

2 tablespoons instant white chocolate pudding mix

2 tablespoons instant espresso powder

1 tablespoon salted caramel chocolate chips, cut up

Preparation:

1. In a high-powered blender, put in protein shake, pudding mix, and espresso powder and process to form a smooth mixture. 2. Transfer the blended mixture into an empty Ninja CREAMi pint container. 3. Cover the container with the storage lid and freeze for 24 hours. 4. After 24 hours, take off the lid from container and arrange into the outer bowl of Ninja CREAMi. 5. Install the "Creamerizer Paddle" onto the lid of outer bowl. 6. Then rotate the lid clockwise to lock. 7. Press "Power" button to turn on the unit. 8. Then press "ICE CREAM" button. 9. When the program is completed, with a spoon, create a 1½-inch wide hole in the center that reaches the bottom of the pint container. 10. Add chocolate chips in the hole and press "MIX-IN" button. 11. When the program is completed, turn the outer bowl and release it from the machine. 12. Transfer the ice cream into serving bowls and enjoy immediately.

Nutritional Information per Serving:

Calories: 369 |Fat: 4.1g|Sat Fat: 1.1g|Carbohydrates: 50.6g|Fiber: 0.3g|Sugar: 37.3g|Protein: 34.4g

Fresh Strawberry Banana Ice Cream

Preparation Time: 10 minutes | Servings: 4

Ingredients:

1 (11.5 ounce) bottle strawberry protein shake

1 small banana, peel removed

2 fresh whole strawberries

½ cup fresh strawberries, cut up

Preparation:

1. In a high-powered blender, put in protein shake, banana and 2 strawberries and process to form a smooth mixture. 2. Transfer the blended mixture into an empty Ninja CREAMi pint container. 3. Cover the container with the storage lid and freeze for 24 hours. 4. After 24 hours, take off the lid from container and arrange into the outer bowl of Ninja CREAMi. 5. Install the "Creamerizer Paddle" onto the lid of outer bowl. 6. Then rotate the lid clockwise to lock. 7. Press "Power" button to turn on the unit. 8. Then press "LITE ICE CREAM" button. 9. When the program is completed, with a spoon, create a 1½-inch wide hole in the center that reaches the bottom of the pint container. 10. Add cut up strawberries in the hole and press "MIX-IN" button. 11. When the program is completed, turn the outer bowl and release it from the machine. 12. Transfer the ice cream into serving bowls and enjoy immediately.

Nutritional Information per Serving:

Calories: 31 |Fat: 2.5g|Sat Fat: 0g|Carbohydrates: 46.7g|Fiber: 3.4g|Sugar: 36.6g|Protein: 35.3g

Chocolate Chips Cherry Ice Cream

Preparation Time: 15 minutes | Servings: 4

Ingredients:

½ cup frozen cherries, thawed and squeezed
½ cup granulated sugar
1 cup whole milk
½ teaspoon vanilla extract

½ teaspoon strawberry extract
⅓ cup heavy cream
⅓ cup chocolate chips

Preparation:

1. In a high-powered blender, put in cherries and remaining ingredients except for chocolate chips and process to form a smooth mixture. 2. Transfer the blended mixture into an empty Ninja CREAMi pint container. 3. Put in heavy cream and blend to incorporate. 4. Cover the container with the storage lid and freeze for 24 hours. 5. After 24 hours, take off the lid from container and arrange into the outer bowl of Ninja CREAMi. 6. Install the "Creamerizer Paddle" onto the lid of outer bowl. 7. Then rotate the lid clockwise to lock. 8. Press "Power" button to turn on the unit. 9. Then press "ICE CREAM" button. 10. When the program is completed, with a spoon, create a 1½-inch wide hole in the center that reaches the bottom of the pint container. 11. Add chocolate chips in the hole and press "MIX-IN" button. 12. When the program is completed, turn the outer bowl and release it from the machine. 13. Transfer the ice cream into serving bowls and enjoy immediately.

Nutritional Information per Serving:

Calories: 250 |Fat: 9.9g|Sat Fat: 6.4g|Carbohydrates: 38.6g|Fiber: 0.8g|Sugar: 37.3g|Protein: 3.4g

Chocolate Chips Yogurt Ice Cream

Preparation Time: 10 minute | Servings: 4

Ingredients:

1 cup milk
½ cup milk yogurt
¼ cup unsweetened creamer

½ teaspoon vanilla extract
1 tablespoon whipping cream
3 teaspoons mini chocolate chips

Preparation:

1. In an empty Ninja CREAMi pint container, put in milk, yogurt, creamer, vanilla extract and whipping cream and blend to incorporate. 2. Cover the container with storage lid and freeze for 24 hours. 3. After 24 hours, take off the lid from container and arrange into the outer bowl of Ninja CREAMi. 4. Install the "Creamerizer Paddle" onto the lid of outer bowl. 5. Then rotate the lid clockwise to lock. 6. Press "Power" button to turn on the unit. 7. Then press "ICE CREAM" button. 8. When the program is completed, with a spoon, create a 1½-inch wide hole in the center that reaches the bottom of the pint container. 9. Put in chocolate chips in the hole and press "MIX-IN" button. 10. When the program is completed, turn the outer bowl and release it from the machine. 11. Transfer the ice cream into serving bowls and enjoy immediately.

Nutritional Information per Serving:

Calories: 94 |Fat: 4.6g|Sat Fat: 2.8g|Carbohydrates: 7.9g|Fiber: 0.1g|Sugar: 7.3g|Protein: 5g

Coconut Peach Ice Cream

Preparation Time: 15 minutes | Servings: 4

Ingredients:

1¼ cups heavy cream

½ cup canned peaches, cut into small pieces

1 tablespoon coconut, toasted

1 tablespoon fresh peach, peeled, pitted and chopped

Preparation:

1. In an empty Ninja CREAMi pint container, put in coconut cream and ½ cup of peach tidbits and blend to incorporate. 2. Cover the container with storage lid and freeze for 24 hours. 3. After 24 hours, take off the lid from container and arrange into the outer bowl of Ninja CREAMi. 4. Install the "Creamerizer Paddle" onto the lid of outer bowl. 5. Then rotate the lid clockwise to lock. 6. Press "Power" button to turn on the unit. 7. Then press "ICE CREAM" button. 8. When the program is completed, with a spoon, create a 1½-inch wide hole in the center that reaches the bottom of the pint container. 9. Put in coconut and chopped peach in the hole and press "MIX-IN" button. 10. When the program is completed, turn the outer bowl and release it from the machine. 11. Transfer the ice cream into serving bowls and enjoy immediately.

Nutritional Information per Serving:

Calories: 141 |Fat: 14.4g|Sat Fat: 9g|Carbohydrates: 3g|Fiber: 0.4g|Sugar: 1.9g|Protein: 1g

Simple Chocolate Chips Ice Cream

Preparation Time: 10 minutes | Cooking Time: 10 seconds | Servings: 4

Ingredients:

1 tablespoon cream cheese

⅓ cup granulated sugar

1 teaspoon vanilla extract

¾ cup heavy cream

1 cup whole milk

¼ cup mini chocolate chips

Preparation:

1. In a large-sized, microwave-safe bowl, put in cream cheese and microwave for 10 seconds. 2. Put in sugar and vanilla extract and whisk to form a frosting mixture. 3. Slowly put in the heavy cream and milk and whisk to incorporate thoroughly. 4. Transfer the blended mixture into an empty Ninja CREAMi pint container. 5. Cover the container with the storage lid and freeze for 24 hours. 6. After 24 hours, take off the lid from container and arrange into the outer bowl of Ninja CREAMi. 7. Install the "Creamerizer Paddle" onto the lid of outer bowl. 8. Then rotate the lid clockwise to lock. 9. Press "Power" button to turn on the unit. 10. Then press "ICE CREAM" button. 11. When the program is completed, with a spoon, create a 1½-inch wide hole in the center that reaches the bottom of the pint container. 12. Add chocolate chips in the hole and press "MIX-IN" button. 13. When the program is completed, turn the outer bowl and release it from the machine. 14. Transfer the ice cream into serving bowls and enjoy immediately.

Nutritional Information per Serving:

Calories: 245 |Fat: 14.3g|Sat Fat: 9.1g|Carbohydrates: 26.5g|Fiber: 0.4g|Sugar: 25.5g|Protein: 3.4g

Chocolate Sea Salt Ice Cream

Preparation Time: 15 minutes | Cooking Time: 7 minutes | Servings: 4

Ingredients:

2 cups whole milk
½ cup sugar
1 teaspoon vanilla extract

Pinch of sea salt
1 ounce chocolate chips
2 teaspoons butter

Preparation:

1. In a medium saucepan, put in milk and sugar and whisk to incorporate. 2. Place saucepan on burner at around medium heat and cook for around 3-5 minutes, stirring continuously. 3. Take off the pan of milk mixture from burner and whisk in vanilla extract and salt. 4. Transfer the blended mixture into an empty Ninja CREAMi pint container. 5. Place the container into an ice bath to cool. 6. After cooling, cover the container with the storage lid and freeze for 24 hours. 7. After 24 hours, take off the lid from container and arrange into the outer bowl of Ninja CREAMi. 8. Install the "Creamerizer Paddle" onto the lid of outer bowl. 9. Then rotate the lid clockwise to lock. 10. Press "Power" button to turn on the unit. 11. Then press "ICE CREAM" button. 12. Meanwhile, in a medium-sized microwave-safe bowl, put in chocolate chips and butter and microwave on high for around 2 minutes, stirring after every 20 seconds. 13. Take off the bowl from microwave and blend until smooth. 14. Let the chocolate mixture to cool thoroughly. 15. When the program is completed, with a spoon, create a 1½-inch wide hole in the center that reaches the bottom of the pint container. 16. Add chocolate mixture in the hole and press "MIX-IN" button. 17. When the program is completed, turn the outer bowl and release it from the machine. 18. Transfer the ice cream into serving bowls and enjoy immediately.

Nutritional Information per Serving:

Calories: 225 |Fat: 8g|Sat Fat: 5g|Carbohydrates: 34.9g|Fiber: 0.2g|Sugar: 35.2g|Protein: 4.5g

Chocolate Protein Peanut Butter Ice Cream

Preparation Time: 10 minutes | Servings: 4

Ingredients:

1 (11.5 ounce) bottle chocolate protein shake

2 tablespoons instant chocolate fudge pudding mix

1 teaspoon cocoa powder

2 tablespoons peanut butter powder

3 peanut butter cups

Preparation:

1. In a high-powered blender, put in protein shake, fudge pudding mix, cocoa powder and peanut butter powder and process to form a smooth mixture. 2. Transfer the blended mixture into an empty Ninja CREAMi pint container. 3. Cover the container with the storage lid and freeze for 24 hours. 4. After 24 hours, take off the lid from container and arrange into the outer bowl of Ninja CREAMi. 5. Install the "Creamerizer Paddle" onto the lid of outer bowl. 6. Then rotate the lid clockwise to lock. 7. Press "Power" button to turn on the unit. 8. Then press "LITE ICE CREAM" button. 9. When the program is completed, with a spoon, create a 1½-inch wide hole in the center that reaches the bottom of the pint container. 10. Add peanut butter cups in the hole and press "MIX-IN" button. 11. When the program is completed, turn the outer bowl and release it from the machine. 12. Transfer the ice cream into serving bowls and enjoy immediately.

Nutritional Information per Serving:

Calories: 487 |Fat: 12.1g|Sat Fat: 5.9g|Carbohydrates: 57.6g|Fiber: 1.4g|Sugar: 41.1g|Protein: 39.8g

Cherry Pie Cookie Ice Cream

Preparation Time: 10 minutes | Cooking Time: 10 seconds | Servings: 4

Ingredients:

1 tablespoon cream cheese, softened

2 tablespoons brown sugar

½ teaspoon ground cinnamon

⅛ teaspoon ground ginger

⅛ teaspoon ground nutmeg

Pinch of ground cloves

½ cup heavy cream

¼ cup whole milk

1 cup canned cherry pie filling

¼-½ cup sugar cookies, chopped

Preparation:

1. In a large-sized microwave-safe bowl, put in the cream cheese and microwave on High for about 10 seconds. 2. Take off from the microwave and blend until smooth. 3. Put in brown sugar and spices and with a wire whisk, whisk until the mixture looks like frosting. 4. In a separate large-sized bowl, put in heavy cream, milk, and cherry pie filling and with an immersion blender, whip until apples are chopped into small pieces. 5. Gradually Put in milk mixture into the bowl of sugar mixture and whisk until blended thoroughly. 6. Transfer the blended mixture into an empty Ninja CREAMi pint container. 7. Place the container into an ice bath to cool. 8. After cooling, cover the container with the storage lid and freeze for 24 hours. 9. After 24 hours, take off the lid from container and arrange into the outer bowl of Ninja CREAMi. 10. Install the "Creamerizer Paddle" onto the lid of outer bowl. 11. Then rotate the lid clockwise to lock. 12. Press "Power" button to turn on the unit. 13. Then press "ICE CREAM" button. 14. When the program is completed, with a spoon, create a 1½-inch wide hole in the center that reaches the bottom of the pint container. 15. Put in chopped cookies in the hole and press "MIX-IN" button. 16. When the program is completed, turn the outer bowl and release it from the machine. 17. Transfer the ice cream into serving bowls and enjoy immediately. 18. Transfer the ice cream into serving bowls and enjoy immediately.

Nutritional Information per Serving:

Calories: 384 |Fat: 19g|Sat Fat: 10.3g|Carbohydrates: 52.1g|Fiber: 0.9g|Sugar: 34.4g|Protein: 3g

Homemade Double Chocolate Ice Cream

Preparation Time: 14 minutes | Servings: 4

Ingredients:

1 tablespoon cream cheese, softened
⅓ cup granulated sugar
2 tablespoons unsweetened cocoa powder
1 teaspoon almond extract

1 cup whole milk
¾ cup heavy cream
4 tablespoons mini chocolate chips

Preparation:

1. In a large microwave-safe bowl, put in the cream cheese and microwave on High for about 10 seconds. 2. Take off from the microwave and blend until smooth. 3. Put in sugar, cocoa powder and almond extract and with a wire whisk, beat until the mixture looks like frosting. 4. Slowly Put in milk and heavy cream and whisk to incorporate thoroughly. 5. Transfer the blended mixture into an empty Ninja CREAMi pint container. 6. Cover the container with storage lid and freeze for 24 hours. 7. After 24 hours, take off the lid from container and arrange into the outer bowl of Ninja CREAMi. 8. Install the "Creamerizer Paddle" onto the lid of outer bowl. 9. Then rotate the lid clockwise to lock. 10. Press "Power" button to turn on the unit. 11. Then press "ICE CREAM" button. 12. When the program is completed, with a spoon, create a 1½-inch wide hole in the center that reaches the bottom of the pint container. 13. Put in chocolate chips into the hole and press "MIX-IN" button. 14. When the program is completed, turn the outer bowl and release it from the machine. 15. Transfer the ice cream into serving bowls and enjoy immediately.

Nutritional Information per Serving:

Calories: 251 |Fat: 14.7g|Sat Fat: 9.3g|Carbohydrates: 28g|Fiber: 1.3g|Sugar: 25.5g|Protein: 3.9g

Strawberry Pudding Cookies Ice Cream

Preparation Time: 15 minutes | Cooking Time: 5 minutes | Servings: 4

Ingredients:

1 cup fresh strawberries, chopped

¼ cup plus 1 teaspoon sugar, divided

½ teaspoon lime juice

1 cup milk

½ cup half-and-half

2 tablespoons instant banana pudding mix

2 sugar cookies, crushed

1 teaspoon butter, melted

Preparation:

1. For pie filling: in a small-sized saucepan, put in the strawberries, ¼ cup of sugar, and lime juice on burner at around medium heat. 2. Cook for about 5 minutes, stirring continuously. 3. Take off the pan of filling from burner and set aside to cool. 4. In an empty Ninja CREAMi pint container, put in milk, half-and-half and pudding mix and with a wire whisk, whisk to incorporate thoroughly. 5. Put in filling mixture and blend to incorporate thoroughly. 6. Cover the container with storage lid and freeze for 24 hours. 7. After 24 hours, take off the lid from container and arrange into the outer bowl of Ninja CREAMi. 8. Install the "Creamerizer Paddle" onto the lid of outer bowl. 9. Then rotate the lid clockwise to lock. 10. Press "Power" button to turn on the unit. 11. Then press "ICE CREAM" button. 12. Meanwhile, in a medium-sized bowl, put in sugar cookies, butter and remaining sugar and blend to incorporate thoroughly. 13. When the program is completed, with a spoon, create a 1½-inch wide hole in the center that reaches the bottom of the pint container. 14. Put in cracker mixture in the hole and press "MIX-IN" button. 15. When the program is completed, turn the outer bowl and release it from the machine. 16. Transfer the ice cream into serving bowls and enjoy immediately.

Nutritional Information per Serving:

Calories: 257 |Fat: 12.1g|Sat Fat: 6.7g|Carbohydrates: 235.4g|Fiber: 0.7g|Sugar: 25.7g|Protein: 4.4g

Green Peppermint Chocolate Chip Ice Cream

Preparation Time: 10 minutes | Servings: 4

Ingredients:

1 (11.5 ounce) bottle vanilla protein shake
2 tablespoons sugar
1 teaspoon vanilla bean paste
½ teaspoon peppermint extract

¼ teaspoon guar gum
4 drops green food coloring
2 tablespoons chocolate chips, cut up

Preparation:

1. In a high-powered blender, put in protein shake, sugar, vanilla bean paste, peppermint extract, guar gum and food coloring and process to form a smooth mixture. 2. Transfer the blended mixture into an empty Ninja CREAMi pint container. 3. Cover the container with the storage lid and freeze for 24 hours. 4. After 24 hours, take off the lid from container and arrange into the outer bowl of Ninja CREAMi. 5. Install the "Creamerizer Paddle" onto the lid of outer bowl. 6. Then rotate the lid clockwise to lock. 7. Press "Power" button to turn on the unit. 8. Then press "ICE CREAM" button. 9. When the program is completed, with a spoon, create a 1½-inch wide hole in the center that reaches the bottom of the pint container. 10. Add chocolate chips in the hole and press "MIX-IN" button. 11. When the program is completed, turn the outer bowl and release it from the machine. 12. Transfer the ice cream into serving bowls and enjoy immediately.

Nutritional Information per Serving:

Calories: 357 |Fat: 3.9g|Sat Fat: 1.1g|Carbohydrates: 49.1g|Fiber: 0.4g|Sugar: 39.1g|Protein: 33g

Butter Sandwich Cookies Ice Cream

Preparation Time: 15 minutes | Cooking Time: 10 seconds | Servings: 4

Ingredients:

1 tablespoon cream cheese

⅓ cup granulated sugar

1 teaspoon almond extract

1 cup whole milk

¾ cup heavy cream

3 butter cream sandwich cookies, broken

Preparation:

1. In a large-sized microwave-safe bowl, put in the cream cheese and microwave on High for about 10 seconds. 2. Take off from the microwave and blend until smooth. 3. Put in sugar and almond extract and with a wire whisk, beat until the mixture looks like frosting. 4. Slowly Put in milk and heavy cream and whisk until blended thoroughly. 5. Transfer the blended mixture into an empty Ninja CREAMi pint container. 6. Cover the container with storage lid and freeze for 24 hours. 7. After 24 hours, take off the lid from container and arrange into the outer bowl of Ninja CREAMi. 8. Install the "Creamerizer Paddle" onto the lid of outer bowl. 9. Then rotate the lid clockwise to lock. 10. Press "Power" button to turn on the unit. 11. Then press "ICE CREAM" button. 12. When the program is completed, with a spoon, create a 1½-inch wide hole in the center that reaches the bottom of the pint container. 13. Put in crushed cookies in the hole and press "MIX-IN" button. 14. When the program is completed, turn the outer bowl and release it from the machine. 15. Transfer the ice cream into serving bowls and enjoy immediately.

Nutritional Information per Serving:

Calories: 286 |Fat: 15.7g|Sat Fat: 7.6g|Carbohydrates: 34.5g|Fiber: 0.8g|Sugar: 26g|Protein: 4.1g

Cheese Pecan Ice Cream

Preparation Time: 10 minutes | Cooking Time: 5 minutes | Servings: 4

Ingredients:

1 cup heavy cream

½ cup whole milk

¼ cup maple syrup

2 ounces ricotta cheese

2 tablespoons raspberry jam

2 tablespoons lime curd

¼ cup pecans, chopped

Preparation:

1. In a small-sized saucepan, put in cream, milk, and maple syrup on burner at around medium heat and cook until heated through, stirring continuously. 2. Add in the ricotta cheese and blend to incorporate thoroughly. 3. Transfer the blended mixture into an empty Ninja CREAMi pint container. 4. Place the container into an ice bath to cool. 5. After cooling, cover the container with the storage lid and freeze for 24 hours. 6. After 24 hours, take off the lid from container and arrange into the outer bowl of Ninja CREAMi. 7. Install the "Creamerizer Paddle" onto the lid of outer bowl. 8. Then rotate the lid clockwise to lock. 9. Press "Power" button to turn on the unit. 10. Then press "ICE CREAM" button. 11. When the program is completed, with a spoon, create a 1½-inch wide hole in the center that reaches the bottom of the pint container. 12. Put in jam, lime curd and pecans in the hole and press "MIX-IN" button. 13. When the program is completed, turn the outer bowl and release it from the machine. 14. Transfer the ice cream into serving bowls and enjoy immediately.

Nutritional Information per Serving:

Calories: 356 |Fat: 39.3g|Sat Fat: 10.3g|Carbohydrates: 27.4g|Fiber: 1.7g|Sugar: 27.4g|Protein: 5.4g

Peanut Butter Ice Cream

Preparation Time: 10 minutes | Cooking Time: 10 seconds | Servings: 4

Ingredients:

1 tablespoon cream cheese

⅓ cup granulated sugar

1 teaspoon vanilla extract

¾ cup heavy cream

1 cup whole milk

¼ cup peanut butter chips

Preparation:

1. In a large-sized, microwave-safe bowl, put in cream cheese and microwave for 10 seconds. 2. Put in sugar and vanilla extract and whisk to form a frosting mixture. 3. Slowly put in the heavy cream and milk and whisk to incorporate thoroughly. 4. Transfer the blended mixture into an empty Ninja CREAMi pint container. 5. Cover the container with the storage lid and freeze for 24 hours. 6. After 24 hours, take off the lid from container and arrange into the outer bowl of Ninja CREAMi. 7. Install the "Creamerizer Paddle" onto the lid of outer bowl. 8. Then rotate the lid clockwise to lock. 9. Press "Power" button to turn on the unit. 10. Then press "ICE CREAM" button. 11. When the program is completed, with a spoon, create a 1½-inch wide hole in the center that reaches the bottom of the pint container. 12. Add peanut butter chips in the hole and press "MIX-IN" button. 13. When the program is completed, turn the outer bowl and release it from the machine. 14. Transfer the ice cream into serving bowls and enjoy immediately.

Nutritional Information per Serving:

Calories: 259 |Fat: 15.2g|Sat Fat: 9.9g|Carbohydrates: 29.3g|Fiber: 0g|Sugar: 29g|Protein: 2.6g

Peppermint & Chocolate Ice Cream

Preparation Time: 10 minutes | Cooking Time: 10 seconds | Servings: 4

Ingredients:

1 tablespoon cream cheese

⅓ cup sugar

1 teaspoon peppermint extract

1 cup whole milk

¾ cup heavy cream

¼ cup chocolate, finely cut up

Preparation:

1. In a large-sized, microwave-safe bowl, put in cream cheese and microwave for 10 seconds. 2. Put in sugar and peppermint extract and whisk to form a frosting mixture. 3. Slowly put in the heavy cream and milk and whisk to incorporate thoroughly. 4. Transfer the blended mixture into an empty Ninja CREAMi pint container. 5. Cover the container with the storage lid and freeze for 24 hours. 6. After 24 hours, take off the lid from container and arrange into the outer bowl of Ninja CREAMi. 7. Install the "Creamerizer Paddle" onto the lid of outer bowl. 8. Then rotate the lid clockwise to lock. 9. Press "Power" button to turn on the unit. 10. Then press "ICE CREAM" button. 11. When the program is completed, with a spoon, create a 1½-inch wide hole in the center that reaches the bottom of the pint container. 12. Add chocolate pieces in the hole and press "MIX-IN" button. 13. When the program is completed, turn the outer bowl and release it from the machine. 14. Transfer the ice cream into serving bowls and enjoy immediately.

Nutritional Information per Serving:

Calories: 245 |Fat: 14.3g|Sat Fat: 9.1g|Carbohydrates: 26.5g|Fiber: 0.4g|Sugar: 25.5g|Protein: 3.4g

Strawberry & Graham Cracker Ice Cream

Preparation Time: 10 minutes | Servings: 4

Ingredients:

1 (11.5 ounce) bottle strawberry protein shake
½ cup cottage cheese
¼ teaspoon strawberry extract

½ cup fresh strawberries, cut up
½ graham cracker, broken into pieces

Preparation:

1. In a high-powered blender, put in protein shake, cottage cheese, and strawberry extract and process to form a smooth mixture. 2. Transfer the blended mixture into an empty Ninja CREAMi pint container. 3. Cover the container with the storage lid and freeze for 24 hours. 4. After 24 hours, take off the lid from container and arrange into the outer bowl of Ninja CREAMi. 5. Install the "Creamerizer Paddle" onto the lid of outer bowl. 6. Then rotate the lid clockwise to lock. 7. Press "Power" button to turn on the unit. 8. Then press "ICE CREAM" button. 9. When the program is completed, with a spoon, create a 1½-inch wide hole in the center that reaches the bottom of the pint container. 10. Add strawberries and graham cracker in the hole and press "MIX-IN" button. 11. When the program is completed, turn the outer bowl and release it from the machine. 12. Transfer the ice cream into serving bowls and enjoy immediately.

Nutritional Information per Serving:

Calories: 83 |Fat: 1.7g|Sat Fat: 0.9g|Carbohydrates: 4.5g|Fiber: 0.4g|Sugar: 2.4g|Protein: 12.1g

Caramel Banana Chocolate Chips Ice Cream

Preparation Time: 10 minutes | Servings: 4

Ingredients:

1 (11.5 ounce) bottle caramel protein shake

1 small banana, peel removed

1 tablespoon chocolate chips, cut up

Preparation:

1. In a high-powered blender, put in protein shake and banana and process to form a smooth mixture. 2. Transfer the blended mixture into an empty Ninja CREAMi pint container. 3. Cover the container with the storage lid and freeze for 24 hours. 4. After 24 hours, take off the lid from container and arrange into the outer bowl of Ninja CREAMi. 5. Install the "Creamerizer Paddle" onto the lid of outer bowl. 6. Then rotate the lid clockwise to lock. 7. Press "Power" button to turn on the unit. 8. Then press "LITE ICE CREAM" button. 9. When the program is completed, with a spoon, create a 1½-inch wide hole in the center that reaches the bottom of the pint container. 10. Add chocolate chips in the hole and press "MIX-IN" button. 11. When the program is completed, turn the outer bowl and release it from the machine. 12. Transfer the ice cream into serving bowls and enjoy immediately.

Nutritional Information per Serving:

Calories: 369 |Fat: 3.9g|Sat Fat: 2.1g|Carbohydrates: 19.4g|Fiber: 0.8g|Sugar: 4.4g|Protein: 36.9g

Granola Peach Ice Cream

Preparation Time: 10 minutes | Servings: 4

Ingredients:

1 (15¼-ounce) can peaches in heavy syrup, drained and divided
12 ounces peach yogurt
1 teaspoon sugar

½ teaspoon vanilla extract
¼ teaspoon ground cinnamon
¼ cup honey granola

Preparation:

1. Place half of peaches, yogurt, sugar, vanilla extract and cinnamon in an empty Ninja CREAMi pint container and blend to incorporate. 2. Cover the container with the storage lid and freeze for 24 hours. 3. After 24 hours, take off the lid from container and arrange into the outer bowl of Ninja CREAMi. 4. Install the "Creamerizer Paddle" onto the lid of outer bowl. 5. Then rotate the lid clockwise to lock. 6. Press "Power" button to turn on the unit. 7. Then press "LITE ICE CREAM" button. 8. When the program is completed, with a spoon, create a 1½-inch wide hole in the center that reaches the bottom of the pint container. 9. Add remaining peaches and granola in the hole and press "MIX-IN" button. 10. When the program is completed, turn the outer bowl and release it from the machine. 11. Transfer the ice cream into serving bowls and enjoy immediately.

Nutritional Information per Serving:

Calories: 322 |Fat: 3.4g|Sat Fat: 1.4g|Carbohydrates: 66.1g|Fiber: 9.4g|Sugar: 63g|Protein: 10.9g

Cinnamon Raisin Oatmeal Cookies Ice Cream

Preparation Time: 10 minutes | Servings: 4

Ingredients:

1 cup milk
½ cup brown sugar
2 tablespoons cream cheese

¼ teaspoon ground cinnamon
¼ cup oatmeal raisin cookies, crumbled

Preparation:

1. In a high-powered blender, put in milk, brown sugar, cream cheese and cinnamon and process to form a smooth mixture. 2. Transfer the blended mixture into an empty Ninja CREAMi pint container. 3. Cover the container with the storage lid and freeze for 24 hours. 4. After 24 hours, take off the lid from container and arrange into the outer bowl of Ninja CREAMi. 5. Install the "Creamerizer Paddle" onto the lid of outer bowl. 6. Then rotate the lid clockwise to lock. 7. Press "Power" button to turn on the unit. 8. Then press "ICE CREAM" button. 9. When the program is completed, with a spoon, create a 1½-inch wide hole in the center that reaches the bottom of the pint container. 10. Add cookies in the hole and press "MIX-IN" button. 11. When the program is completed, turn the outer bowl and release it from the machine. 12. Transfer the ice cream into serving bowls and enjoy immediately.

Nutritional Information per Serving:

Calories: 185 |Fat: 5.6g|Sat Fat: 1.9g|Carbohydrates: 31.5g|Fiber: 0.8g|Sugar: 26.4g|Protein: 3.9g

Chocolate Cashew Ice Cream

Preparation Time: 15 minutes | Cooking Time: 7 minutes | Servings: 4

Ingredients:

1 cup coconut milk

1 cup cashew milk

½ cup sugar

1 teaspoon vanilla extract

¼ teaspoon salt

1-ounce chocolate chips

2 teaspoons coconut oil

Preparation:

1. In a medium saucepan, put in coconut milk, cashew milk and sugar and whisk to incorporate. 2. Place saucepan on burner at around medium heat and cook for around 3-5 minutes, stirring continuously. 3. Take off the pan of milk mixture from burner and whisk in vanilla extract and salt. 4. Transfer the blended mixture into an empty Ninja CREAMi pint container. 5. Place the container into an ice bath to cool. 6. After cooling, cover the container with the storage lid and freeze for 24 hours. 7. After 24 hours, take off the lid from container and arrange into the outer bowl of Ninja CREAMi. 8. Install the "Creamerizer Paddle" onto the lid of outer bowl. 9. Then rotate the lid clockwise to lock. 10. Press "Power" button to turn on the unit. 11. Then press "ICE CREAM" button. 12. Meanwhile, in a medium-sized microwave-safe bowl, put in chocolate chips and coconut oil and microwave on high for around 2 minutes, stirring after every 20 seconds. 13. Take off the bowl from microwave and stir until smooth. 14. Let the chocolate mixture to cool thoroughly. 15. When the program is completed, with a spoon, create a 1½-inch wide hole in the center that reaches the bottom of the pint container. 16. Add chocolate mixture in the hole and press "MIX-IN" button. 17. When the program is completed, turn the outer bowl and release it from the machine. 18. Transfer the ice cream into serving bowls and enjoy immediately.

Nutritional Information per Serving:

Calories: 299 |Fat: 19.2g|Sat Fat: 16.1g|Carbohydrates: 32.9g|Fiber: 1.6g|Sugar: 30.8g|Protein: 1.9g

Zucchini & Chocolate Chips Ice Cream

Preparation Time: 15 minutes | Servings: 4

Ingredients:

½ cup frozen zucchini, thawed and squeezed dry
½ cup granulated sugar
1 cup whole milk
½ teaspoon lemon extract

½ teaspoon raspberry extract
4 drops green food coloring
⅓ cup heavy cream
⅓ cup chocolate chips

Preparation:

1. In a high-powered blender, put in zucchini and remaining ingredients except for chocolate chips and process to form a smooth mixture. 2. Transfer the blended mixture into an empty Ninja CREAMi pint container. 3. Put in heavy cream and blend to incorporate. 4. Cover the container with the storage lid and freeze for 24 hours. 5. After 24 hours, take off the lid from container and arrange into the outer bowl of Ninja CREAMi. 6. Install the "Creamerizer Paddle" onto the lid of outer bowl. 7. Then rotate the lid clockwise to lock. 8. Press "Power" button to turn on the unit. 9. Then press "ICE CREAM" button. 10. When the program is completed, with a spoon, create a 1½-inch wide hole in the center that reaches the bottom of the pint container. 11. Add chocolate chips in the hole and press "MIX-IN" button. 12. When the program is completed, turn the outer bowl and release it from the machine. 13. Transfer the ice cream into serving bowls and enjoy immediately.

Nutritional Information per Serving:

Calories: 245 |Fat: 9.9g|Sat Fat: 6.4g|Carbohydrates: 37g|Fiber: 0.6g|Sugar: 35.8g|Protein: 3.4g

Lemon Honey Sorbet

Preparation Time: 10 minutes | Servings: 4

Ingredients:

1 cup warm water

½ cup granulated sugar

1 tablespoon honey

½ cup lemon juice

Preparation:

1. In a large-sized bowl, put in warm water, sugar and honey and whisk to incorporate thoroughly. 2. Add lemon juice and whisk to incorporate thoroughly. 3. Transfer the blended mixture into an empty Ninja CREAMi pint container. 4. Cover the container with storage lid and freeze for 24 hours. 5. After 24 hours, take off the lid from container and arrange into the outer bowl of Ninja CREAMi. 6. Install the "Creamerizer Paddle" onto the lid of outer bowl. 7. Then rotate the lid clockwise to lock. 8. Press "Power" button to turn on the unit. 9. Then press "SORBET" button. 10. When the program is completed, turn the outer bowl and release it from the machine. 11. Transfer the sorbet into serving bowls and enjoy immediately.

Nutritional Information per Serving:

Calories: 117 |Fat: 0.2g|Sat Fat: 0.2g|Carbohydrates: 30g|Fiber: 0.1g|Sugar: 30g|Protein: 0.3g

Easy Peach Sorbet

Preparation Time: 10 minutes | Servings: 4

Ingredients:

1 (15-ounce) can peaches in light syrup

Preparation:

1. Place the peach pieces into an empty Ninja CREAMi container to the MAX FILL line. 2. Cover the peach pieces with syrup from the can. 3. Transfer the blended mixture into an empty Ninja CREAMi pint container. 4. Cover the container with storage lid and freeze for 24 hours. 5. After 24 hours, take off the lid from container and arrange into the outer bowl of Ninja CREAMi. 6. Install the "Creamerizer Paddle" onto the lid of outer bowl. 7. Then rotate the lid clockwise to lock. 8. Press "Power" button to turn on the unit. 9. Then press "SORBET" button. 10. When the program is completed, turn the outer bowl and release it from the machine. 11. Transfer the sorbet into serving bowls and enjoy immediately.

Nutritional Information per Serving:

Calories: 221 |Fat: 1.5g|Sat Fat: 0g|Carbohydrates: 52.5g|Fiber: 8.6g|Sugar: 52.5g|Protein: 5.3g

Simple Plum Sorbet

Preparation Time: 10 minutes | Servings: 4

Ingredients:

3 cups plums, pitted and chopped

3-4 drops liquid stevia

Preparation:

1. In an empty Ninja CREAMi pint container, place the plums and stevia and with a potato masher, mash thoroughly. 2. Cover the container with storage lid and freeze for 24 hours. 3. After 24 hours, remove the lid from container and arrange into the outer bowl of Ninja CREAMi. 4. Install the "Creamerizer Paddle" onto the lid of outer bowl. 5. Then rotate the lid clockwise to lock. 6. Press "Power" button to turn on the unit. 7. Then press "SORBET" button. 8. When the program is completed, turn the outer bowl and release it from the machine. 9. Transfer the sorbet into serving bowls and serve immediately.

Nutritional Information per Serving:

Calories: 23 |Fat: 0.2g|Sat Fat: 0g|Carbohydrates: 6g|Fiber: 0.7g|Sugar: 5.3g|Protein: 0.4g

Vanilla Mango Sorbet

Preparation Time: 10 minutes | Servings: 4

Ingredients:

1½ cups frozen mango chunks
½ cup mango juice

¼ cup whole milk
1 teaspoon vanilla extract

Preparation:

1. In a high-powered blender, put in mango chunks and remaining ingredients and process to form a smooth mixture. 2. Transfer the blended mixture into an empty Ninja CREAMi pint container. 3. Cover the container with storage lid and freeze for 24 hours. 4. After 24 hours, take off the lid from container and arrange into the outer bowl of Ninja CREAMi. 5. Install the "Creamerizer Paddle" onto the lid of outer bowl. 6. Then rotate the lid clockwise to lock. 7. Press "Power" button to turn on the unit. 8. Then press "SORBET" button. 9. When the program is completed, turn the outer bowl and release it from the machine. 10. Transfer the sorbet into serving bowls and enjoy immediately.

Nutritional Information per Serving:

Calories: 58 |Fat: 0.7g|Sat Fat: 0.3g|Carbohydrates: 12.4g|Fiber: 1g|Sugar: 10g|Protein: 1g

Lime Raspberry Sorbet

Preparation Time: 10 minutes | Servings: 4

Ingredients:

4½ cups fresh raspberries

¼ cup granulated sugar

2 teaspoons lime juice

Preparation:

1. In a high-powered blender, put in raspberries, sugar and lime juice and process to form a smooth mixture. 2. Transfer the blended mixture into an empty Ninja CREAMi pint container. 3. Cover the container with storage lid and freeze for 24 hours. 4. After 24 hours, take off the lid from container and arrange into the outer bowl of Ninja CREAMi. 5. Install the "Creamerizer Paddle" onto the lid of outer bowl. 6. Then rotate the lid clockwise to lock. 7. Press "Power" button to turn on the unit. 8. Then press "SORBET" button. 9. When the program is completed, turn the outer bowl and release it from the machine. 10. Transfer the sorbet into serving bowls and enjoy immediately.

Nutritional Information per Serving:

Calories: 119 |Fat: 0.9g|Sat Fat: 0g|Carbohydrates: 29.2g|Fiber: 9g|Sugar: 18.7g|Protein: 1.7g

Ginger Strawberry Sorbet

Preparation Time: 10 minutes | Servings: 4

Ingredients:

3 cups fresh strawberries

⅓ cup water

⅓ cup sugar

¾ cup ginger ale

Preparation:

1. In a high-speed blender, put in strawberries and remaining ingredients and pulse until smooth. 2. Transfer the blended mixture into an empty Ninja CREAMi pint container. 3. Cover the container with storage lid and freeze for 24 hours. 4. After 24 hours, take off the lid from container and arrange into the outer bowl of Ninja CREAMi. 5. Install the "Creamerizer Paddle" onto the lid of outer bowl. 6. Then rotate the lid clockwise to lock. 7. Press "Power" button to turn on the unit. 8. Then press "SORBET" button. 9. When the program is completed, turn the outer bowl and release it from the machine. 10. Transfer the sorbet into serving bowls and enjoy immediately.

Nutritional Information per Serving:

Calories: 113 |Fat: 0.3g|Sat Fat: 0g|Carbohydrates: 29g|Fiber: 2.2g|Sugar: 25.9g|Protein: 0.7g

Berries Sorbet

Preparation Time: 10 minutes | Servings: 4

Ingredients:

1 pound frozen mixed berries

4¼ ounces caster sugar

1 teaspoon lime juice

Preparation:

1. In a high-powered blender, put in berries and remaining ingredients and process to form a smooth mixture. 2. Transfer the blended mixture into an empty Ninja CREAMi pint container. 3. Cover the container with storage lid and freeze for 24 hours. 4. After 24 hours, take off the lid from container and arrange into the outer bowl of Ninja CREAMi. 5. Install the "Creamerizer Paddle" onto the lid of outer bowl. 6. Then rotate the lid clockwise to lock. 7. Press "Power" button to turn on the unit. 8. Then press "SORBET" button. 9. When the program is completed, turn the outer bowl and release it from the machine. 10. Transfer the sorbet into serving bowls and enjoy immediately.

Nutritional Information per Serving:

Calories: 178 |Fat: 0.4g|Sat Fat: 0g|Carbohydrates: 44g|Fiber: 4.1g|Sugar: 38.2g|Protein: 0.8g

Lemony Tropical Fruit Sorbet

Preparation Time: 10 minutes | Servings: 4

Ingredients:

1 cup frozen pineapple chunks

1 cup frozen mango chunks

1 cup frozen papaya chunks

½ cup full-fat coconut milk

2 tablespoons honey

2 tablespoons fresh lemon juice

1 teaspoon lemon zest

Preparation:

1. In a high-powered blender, put in mango chunks and remaining ingredients and process to form a smooth mixture. 2. Transfer the blended mixture into an empty Ninja CREAMi pint container. 3. Cover the container with storage lid and freeze for 24 hours. 4. After 24 hours, take off the lid from container and arrange into the outer bowl of Ninja CREAMi. 5. Install the "Creamerizer Paddle" onto the lid of outer bowl. 6. Then rotate the lid clockwise to lock. 7. Press "Power" button to turn on the unit. 8. Then press "SORBET" button. 9. When the program is completed, turn the outer bowl and release it from the machine. 10. Transfer the sorbet into serving bowls and enjoy immediately.

Nutritional Information per Serving:

Calories: 109 |Fat: 1.8g|Sat Fat: 1.5g|Carbohydrates: 24.6g|Fiber: 2g|Sugar: 21.3g|Protein: 1g

Fresh Fruity Gelato

Preparation Time: 10 minutes | Servings: 4

Ingredients:

2 cups peaches, peeled, pitted and sliced
2 cup fresh mango, peeled, pitted and sliced
¼ cup pineapple chunks with unsweetened juice

¼ cup fresh orange juice
1 teaspoon maple syrup
½ teaspoon fresh lemon juice

Preparation:

1. In a high-powered blender, put in peaches and remaining ingredients and process to form a smooth mixture. 2. Transfer the blended mixture into an empty Ninja CREAMi pint container. 3. Cover the container with storage lid and freeze for 24 hours. 4. After 24 hours, take off the lid from container and arrange into the outer bowl of Ninja CREAMi. 5. Install the "Creamerizer Paddle" onto the lid of outer bowl. 6. Then rotate the lid clockwise to lock. 7. Press "Power" button to turn on the unit. 8. Then press "SORBET" button. 9. When the program is completed, turn the outer bowl and release it from the machine. 10. Transfer the sorbet into serving bowls and enjoy immediately.

Nutritional Information per Serving:

Calories: 96 |Fat: 0.6g|Sat Fat: 0.1g|Carbohydrates: 23.5g|Fiber: 2.6g|Sugar: 21.6g|Protein: 1.6g

Pear Seltzer Sorbet

Preparation Time: 10 minutes | Servings: 4

Ingredients:

½ cup sangria seltzer
3 tablespoons maple syrup

1 (15¼-ounce) can pear in a heavy syrup, drained

Preparation:

1. In a large-sized bowl, put in the seltzer and maple syrup and whisk blended thoroughly. 2. In an empty Ninja CREAMi pint container, put in the pear pieces and top with agave mixture. 3. Cover the container with storage lid and freeze for 24 hours. 4. After 24 hours, take off the lid from container and arrange into the outer bowl of Ninja CREAMi. 5. Install the "Creamerizer Paddle" onto the lid of outer bowl. 6. Then rotate the lid clockwise to lock. 7. Press "Power" button to turn on the unit. 8. Then press "SORBET" button. 9. When the program is completed, turn the outer bowl and release it from the machine. 10. Transfer the sorbet into serving bowls and enjoy immediately.

Nutritional Information per Serving:

Calories: 126 |Fat: 0.1g|Sat Fat: 0g|Carbohydrates: 30.8g|Fiber: 1.7g|Sugar: 22g|Protein: 0.2g

Pineapple & Mango Coconut Milk Sorbet

Preparation Time: 10 minutes | Servings: 4

Ingredients:

1 cup frozen pineapple chunks

½ cup frozen mango chunks

½ cup pineapple mango Juice

¼ cup unsweetened coconut milk

1 teaspoon pure vanilla extract

Preparation:

1. In a high-powered blender, put in pineapple chunks and remaining ingredients and process to form a smooth mixture. 2. Transfer the blended mixture into an empty Ninja CREAMi pint container. 3. Cover the container with storage lid and freeze for 24 hours. 4. After 24 hours, take off the lid from container and arrange into the outer bowl of Ninja CREAMi. 5. Install the "Creamerizer Paddle" onto the lid of outer bowl. 6. Then rotate the lid clockwise to lock. 7. Press "Power" button to turn on the unit. 8. Then press "SORBET" button. 9. When the program is completed, turn the outer bowl and release it from the machine. 10. Transfer the sorbet into serving bowls and enjoy immediately.

Nutritional Information per Serving:

Calories: 87 |Fat: 3.8g|Sat Fat: 3.2g|Carbohydrates: 13.5g|Fiber: 1.3g|Sugar: 10.6g|Protein: 0.8g

Lime Watermelon Sorbet

Preparation Time: 10 minutes | Servings: 4

Ingredients:

1⅔ cups seedless watermelon chunks

⅓ cup sweetened condensed milk

1 teaspoon lime juice

Pinch of salt

Preparation:

1. In a high-powered blender, put in watermelon and remaining ingredients and process to form a smooth mixture. 2. Transfer the blended mixture into an empty Ninja CREAMi pint container. 3. Cover the container with storage lid and freeze for 24 hours. 4. After 24 hours, take off the lid from container and arrange into the outer bowl of Ninja CREAMi. 5. Install the "Creamerizer Paddle" onto the lid of outer bowl. 6. Then rotate the lid clockwise to lock. 7. Press "Power" button to turn on the unit. 8. Then press "SORBET" button. 9. When the program is completed, turn the outer bowl and release it from the machine. 10. Transfer the sorbet into serving bowls and enjoy immediately.

Nutritional Information per Serving:

Calories: 101 |Fat: 2.3g|Sat Fat: 1.4g|Carbohydrates: 18.7g|Fiber: 0.3g|Sugar: 17.8g|Protein: 2.4g

Tasty Cherry Sorbet

Preparation Time: 10 minutes | Servings: 4

Ingredients:

1 pound frozen cherries, pitted

4¼ ounces caster sugar

1 teaspoon lemon juice

Preparation:

1. In a high-powered blender, put in cherries and remaining ingredients and process to form a smooth mixture. 2. Transfer the blended mixture into an empty Ninja CREAMi pint container. 3. Cover the container with storage lid and freeze for 24 hours. 4. After 24 hours, take off the lid from container and arrange into the outer bowl of Ninja CREAMi. 5. Install the "Creamerizer Paddle" onto the lid of outer bowl. 6. Then rotate the lid clockwise to lock. 7. Press "Power" button to turn on the unit. 8. Then press "SORBET" button. 9. When the program is completed, turn the outer bowl and release it from the machine. 10. Transfer the sorbet into serving bowls and enjoy immediately.

Nutritional Information per Serving:

Calories: 165 |Fat: 0.5g|Sat Fat: 0.1g|Carbohydrates: 42.7g|Fiber: 1.8g|Sugar: 40.4g|Protein: 1.1g

Easy Lime Sorbet

Preparation Time: 10 minutes | Servings: 4

Ingredients:

1 cup warm water

½ cup granulated sugar

1 tablespoon light corn syrup

½ cup lime juice

Preparation:

1. In a large-sized bowl, put in warm water, sugar and corn syrup, and whisk to incorporate thoroughly. 2. Add lime juice and whisk to incorporate thoroughly. 3. Transfer the blended mixture into an empty Ninja CREAMi pint container. 4. Cover the container with storage lid and freeze for 24 hours. 5. After 24 hours, take off the lid from container and arrange into the outer bowl of Ninja CREAMi. 6. Install the "Creamerizer Paddle" onto the lid of outer bowl. 7. Then rotate the lid clockwise to lock. 8. Press "Power" button to turn on the unit. 9. Then press "SORBET" button. 10. When the program is completed, turn the outer bowl and release it from the machine. 11. Transfer the sorbet into serving bowls and enjoy immediately.

Nutritional Information per Serving:

Calories: 114 |Fat: 0.1g|Sat Fat: 0g|Carbohydrates: 30.7g|Fiber: 0.1g|Sugar: 26.7g|Protein: 0.1g

Fresh Raspberry Sorbet

Preparation Time: 10 minutes | Servings: 4

Ingredients:

4½ cups fresh raspberries   ¼ cup granulated sugar

Preparation:

1. In a high-powered blender, put in raspberries and sugar and process to form a smooth mixture. 2. Transfer the blended mixture into an empty Ninja CREAMi pint container. 3. Cover the container with storage lid and freeze for 24 hours. 4. After 24 hours, take off the lid from container and arrange into the outer bowl of Ninja CREAMi. 5. Install the "Creamerizer Paddle" onto the lid of outer bowl. 6. Then rotate the lid clockwise to lock. 7. Press "Power" button to turn on the unit. 8. Then press "SORBET" button. 9. When the program is completed, turn the outer bowl and release it from the machine. 10. Transfer the sorbet into serving bowls and enjoy immediately.

Nutritional Information per Serving:

Calories: 119 |Fat: 0.9g|Sat Fat: 0g|Carbohydrates: 29g|Fiber: 9g|Sugar: 18.6g|Protein: 1.7g

Simple Orange Sorbet

Preparation Time: 10 minutes | Servings: 4

Ingredients:

1 (15-ounce) can mandarin oranges in light syrup   ¼ cup granulated sugar

Preparation:

1. In a high-powered blender, put in oranges and sugar and process to form a smooth mixture. 2. Transfer the blended mixture into an empty Ninja CREAMi pint container. 3. Cover the container with storage lid and freeze for 24 hours. 4. After 24 hours, take off the lid from container and arrange into the outer bowl of Ninja CREAMi. 5. Install the "Creamerizer Paddle" onto the lid of outer bowl. 6. Then rotate the lid clockwise to lock. 7. Press "Power" button to turn on the unit. 8. Then press "SORBET" button. 9. When the program is completed, turn the outer bowl and release it from the machine. 10. Transfer the sorbet into serving bowls and enjoy immediately.

Nutritional Information per Serving:

Calories: 86 |Fat: 0g|Sat Fat: 0g|Carbohydrates: 22.7g|Fiber: 0.7g|Sugar: 21.9g|Protein: 0.7g

Easy Pear Sorbet

Preparation Time: 10 minutes | Servings: 4

Ingredients:

1 (15-ounce) can pear halves in heavy syrup

Preparation:

1. In a high-powered blender, put in pear halves and process to form a smooth mixture. 2. Transfer the blended pear halves into an empty Ninja CREAMi pint container. 3. Cover the container with storage lid and freeze for 24 hours. 4. After 24 hours, take off the lid from container and arrange into the outer bowl of Ninja CREAMi. 5. Install the "Creamerizer Paddle" onto the lid of outer bowl. 6. Then rotate the lid clockwise to lock. 7. Press "Power" button to turn on the unit. 8. Then press "SORBET" button. 9. When the program is completed, turn the outer bowl and release it from the machine. 10. Transfer the sorbet into serving bowls and enjoy immediately.

Nutritional Information per Serving:

Calories: 61 |Fat: 0.2g|Sat Fat: 0g|Carbohydrates: 16.2g|Fiber: 3.3g|Sugar: 10.4g|Protein: 0.4g

Fresh Blueberry Sorbet

Preparation Time: 10 minutes | Servings: 4

Ingredients:

4½ cups fresh blueberries

¼ cup granulated sugar

2 teaspoons lemon juice

Preparation:

1. In a high-powered blender, put in blueberries, sugar and lemon juice and process to form a smooth mixture. 2. Transfer the blended mixture into an empty Ninja CREAMi pint container. 3. Cover the container with storage lid and freeze for 24 hours. 4. After 24 hours, take off the lid from container and arrange into the outer bowl of Ninja CREAMi. 5. Install the "Creamerizer Paddle" onto the lid of outer bowl. 6. Then rotate the lid clockwise to lock. 7. Press "Power" button to turn on the unit. 8. Then press "SORBET" button. 9. When the program is completed, turn the outer bowl and release it from the machine. 10. Transfer the sorbet into serving bowls and enjoy immediately.

Nutritional Information per Serving:

Calories: 141 |Fat: 0.6g|Sat Fat: 0g|Carbohydrates: 36.2g|Fiber: 4g|Sugar: 28.8g|Protein: 1.3g

Chocolate Gelato

Preparation Time: 10 minutes | Cooking Time: 5 minutes | Servings: 4

Ingredients:

1 cup whole milk

¾ cup heavy cream

⅓ cup granulated sugar

⅓ cup dark chocolate chunks

2 egg yolks

2 tablespoons unsweetened cocoa powder

1 teaspoon vanilla extract

Preparation:

1. In a medium-sized saucepan, put in milk and remaining ingredients on burner at around medium heat and cook for around 5 minutes, whisking constantly. 2. Through a fine-mesh strainer, strain the mixture into an empty Ninja CREAMi pint container. 3. Place the container into an ice bath to cool. 4. After cooling, cover the container with the storage lid and freeze for 24 hours. 5. After 24 hours, take off the lid from container and arrange into the outer bowl of Ninja CREAMi. 6. Install the "Creamerizer Paddle" onto the lid of outer bowl. 7. Then rotate the lid clockwise to lock. 8. Press "Power" button to turn on the unit. 9. Then press "GELATO" button. 10. When the program is completed, turn the outer bowl and release it from the machine. 11. Transfer the gelato into serving bowls and serve immediately.

Nutritional Information per Serving:

Calories: 288 |Fat: 17.1g|Sat Fat: 10.3g|Carbohydrates: 30.3g|Fiber: 1.4g|Sugar: 27.3g|Protein: 5.4g

Maple Cacao Gelato

Preparation Time: 10 minutes | Cooking Time: 5 minutes | Servings: 4

Ingredients:

4 egg yolks

⅓ cup maple syrup

1¾ cups full-fat coconut milk

2 tablespoons cacao powder

Preparation:

1. In a medium-sized saucepan, put in egg yolks and remaining ingredients on burner at around medium heat and cook for around 3-5 minutes, stirring continuously. 2. Through a fine-mesh strainer, strain the mixture into an empty Ninja CREAMi pint container. 3. Place the container into an ice bath to cool. 4. After cooling, cover the container with the storage lid and freeze for 24 hours. 5. After 24 hours, take off the lid from container and arrange into the outer bowl of Ninja CREAMi. 6. Install the "Creamerizer Paddle" onto the lid of outer bowl. 7. Then rotate the lid clockwise to lock. 8. Press "Power" button to turn on the unit. 9. Then press "GELATO" button. 10. When the program is completed, turn the outer bowl and release it from the machine. 11. Transfer the gelato into serving bowls and serve immediately.

Nutritional Information per Serving:

Calories: 339 |Fat: 26.1g|Sat Fat: 21.2g|Carbohydrates: 23g|Fiber: 0.8g|Sugar: 17.5g|Protein: 5g

Snickerdoodle Cookie Mix Gelato

Preparation Time: 10 minutes | Cooking Time: 5 minutes | Servings: 4

Ingredients:

1 cup whole milk

¾ cup heavy cream

⅓ cup granulated sugar

¼ cup snickerdoodle cookie mix

2 egg yolks

1 teaspoon vanilla extract

Preparation:

1. In a medium-sized saucepan, put in milk and remaining ingredients on burner at around medium heat and cook for around 5 minutes, whisking constantly. 2. Through a fine-mesh strainer, strain the mixture into an empty Ninja CREAMi pint container. 3. Pour the mixture into a Ninja Creami pint container, ensuring it does not go over the max fill line. 4. Place the container into an ice bath to cool. 5. After cooling, cover the container with the storage lid and freeze for 24 hours. 6. After 24 hours, take off the lid from container and arrange into the outer bowl of Ninja CREAMi. 7. Install the "Creamerizer Paddle" onto the lid of outer bowl. 8. Then rotate the lid clockwise to lock. 9. Press "Power" button to turn on the unit. 10. Then press "GELATO" button. 11. When the program is completed, turn the outer bowl and release it from the machine. 12. Transfer the gelato into serving bowls and serve immediately.

Nutritional Information per Serving:

Calories: 250 |Fat: 12.6g|Sat Fat: 7.1g|Carbohydrates: 27.9g|Fiber: 1.4g|Sugar: 20.1g|Protein: 7.6g

Simple Peanut Butter Cookies Gelato

Preparation Time: 10 minutes | Cooking Time: 5 minutes | Servings: 4

Ingredients:

1 cup whole milk

¾ cup heavy cream

⅓ cup granulated sugar

¼ cup peanut butter cookie mix

2 egg yolks

1 teaspoon vanilla extract

Preparation:

1. In a medium-sized saucepan, put in milk and remaining ingredients on burner at around medium heat and cook for around 5 minutes, whisking constantly. 2. Through a fine-mesh strainer, strain the blended mixture into an empty Ninja CREAMi pint container. 3. Place the container into an ice bath to cool. 4. After cooling, cover the container with the storage lid and freeze for 24 hours. 5. After 24 hours, take off the lid from container and arrange into the outer bowl of Ninja CREAMi. 6. Install the "Creamerizer Paddle" onto the lid of outer bowl. 7. Then rotate the lid clockwise to lock. 8. Press "Power" button to turn on the unit. 9. Then press "GELATO" button. 10. When the program is completed, turn the outer bowl and release it from the machine. 11. Transfer the gelato into serving bowls and enjoy immediately.

Nutritional Information per Serving:

Calories: 258 |Fat: 15g|Sat Fat: 7.7g|Carbohydrates: 27g|Fiber: 0.1g|Sugar: 23.9g|Protein: 4.3g

Sugar Cookie Gelato

Preparation Time: 10 minutes | Cooking Time: 5 minutes | Servings: 4

Ingredients:

1 cup whole milk

¾ cup heavy cream

⅓ cup granulated sugar

¼ cup sugar cookie mix

2 egg yolks

1 teaspoon vanilla extract

Preparation:

1. In a medium-sized saucepan, put in milk and remaining ingredients on burner at around medium heat and cook for around 5 minutes, whisking constantly. 2. Through a fine-mesh strainer, strain the mixture into an empty Ninja CREAMi pint container. 3. Place the container into an ice bath to cool. 4. After cooling, cover the container with the storage lid and freeze for 24 hours. 5. After 24 hours, take off the lid from container and arrange into the outer bowl of Ninja CREAMi. 6. Install the "Creamerizer Paddle" onto the lid of outer bowl. 7. Then rotate the lid clockwise to lock. 8. Press "Power" button to turn on the unit. 9. Then press "GELATO" button. 10. When the program is completed, turn the outer bowl and release it from the machine. 11. Transfer the gelato into serving bowls and serve immediately.

Nutritional Information per Serving:

Calories: 263 |Fat: 13.8g|Sat Fat: 7.4g|Carbohydrates: 31.2g|Fiber: 0g|Sugar: 26.2g|Protein: 4.3g

Flavorful Brownie Gelato

Preparation Time: 10 minutes | Cooking Time: 5 minutes | Servings: 4

Ingredients:

1 cup whole milk

¾ cup heavy cream

⅓ cup granulated sugar

¼ cup brownie mix

2 egg yolks

1 teaspoon vanilla extract

Pinch of salt

Preparation:

1. In a medium-sized saucepan, put in milk and remaining ingredients on burner at around medium heat and cook for around 5 minutes, whisking constantly. 2. Through a fine-mesh strainer, strain the mixture into an empty Ninja CREAMi pint container. 3. Place the container into an ice bath to cool. 4. After cooling, cover the container with the storage lid and freeze for 24 hours. 5. After 24 hours, take off the lid from container and arrange into the outer bowl of Ninja CREAMi. 6. Install the "Creamerizer Paddle" onto the lid of outer bowl. 7. Then rotate the lid clockwise to lock. 8. Press "Power" button to turn on the unit. 9. Then press "GELATO" button. 10. When the program is completed, turn the outer bowl and release it from the machine. 11. Transfer the gelato into serving bowls and serve immediately.

Nutritional Information per Serving:

Calories: 266 |Fat: 14.6g|Sat Fat: 7.5g|Carbohydrates: 31g|Fiber: 0g|Sugar: 20.1g|Protein: 4.3g

Vanilla Mango Gelato

Preparation Time: 10 minutes | Cooking Time: 3 minutes | Servings: 4

Ingredients:

3 large egg yolks

½ cup plus 2 tablespoons granulated sugar, divided

1 tablespoon honey

½ cup crème fraîche

¾ cup whole milk

¼ cup heavy cream

½ teaspoon vanilla extract

1 cup frozen mango chunks

Preparation:

1. In a small-sized saucepan, put in the egg yolks, ½ cup of sugar and honey and whisk until blended thoroughly. 2. Put in crème fraîche, milk, heavy cream and vanilla extract and whisk until blended thoroughly. 3. Place the saucepan on burner at around medium heat and cook for about 2-3 minutes, stirring continuously. 4. Take off the saucepan of milk mixture from burner and through a fine-mesh strainer, strain the blended mixture into an empty Ninja CREAMi pint container. 5. Place the container into an ice bath to cool. 6. After cooling, cover the container with the storage lid and freeze for 24 hours. 7. Meanwhile, in a small-sized saucepan, put in the mango chunks and remaining sugar on burner at around medium heat and cook for about 8 minutes, stirring occasionally and mashing to form a thick jam. 8. Take off the saucepan of mango mixture from burner and transfer the jam into a bowl. 9. Refrigerate the jam until using. 10. After 24 hours, take off the lid from container and arrange the container into the outer bowl of Ninja CREAMi. 11. Install the "Creamerizer Paddle" onto the lid of outer bowl. 12. Then rotate the lid clockwise to lock. 13. Press "Power" button to turn on the unit. 14. Then press "GELATO" button. 15. When the program is completed, with a spoon, create a 1½-inch wide hole in the center that reaches the bottom of the pint container. 16. Put in mango jam into the hole and press "MIX-IN" button. 17. When the program is completed, turn the outer bowl and release it from the machine. 18. Transfer the gelato into serving bowls and enjoy immediately.

Nutritional Information per Serving:

Calories: 249 |Fat: 9.5g|Sat Fat: 4.9g|Carbohydrates: 39.3g|Fiber: 0.7g|Sugar: 38.1g|Protein: 4.2g

Cream Cheese Strawberry Cookies Gelato

Preparation Time: 10 minutes | Cooking Time: 3 minutes | Servings: 4

Ingredients:

4 large egg yolks
3 tablespoons granulated sugar
3 tablespoons strawberry preserves
1 teaspoon vanilla extract

1 cup whole milk
⅓ cup heavy cream
¼ cup cream cheese, softened
3 large shortbread cookies, broken in 1-inch pieces

Preparation:

1. In a small-sized saucepan, put in the egg yolks, sugar, strawberry preserves and vanilla extract and whisk until blended thoroughly. 2. Put in milk, heavy cream and cream cheese and whisk until blended thoroughly. 3. Place the saucepan on burner at around medium heat and cook for about 2-3 minutes, stirring continuously. 4. Take off the saucepan of milk mixture from burner and through a fine-mesh strainer, strain the blended mixture into an empty Ninja CREAMi pint container. 5. Place the container into an ice bath to cool. 6. After cooling, cover the container with the storage lid and freeze for 24 hours. 7. After 24 hours, take off the lid from container and arrange into the outer bowl of Ninja CREAMi. 8. Install the "Creamerizer Paddle" onto the lid of outer bowl. 9. Then rotate the lid clockwise to lock. 10. Press "Power" button to turn on the unit. 11. Then press "GELATO" button. 12. When the program is completed, with a spoon, create a 1½-inch wide hole in the center that reaches the bottom of the pint container. 13. Put in cookies into the hole and press "MIX-IN" button. 14. When the program is completed, turn the outer bowl and release it from the machine. 15. Transfer the gelato into serving bowls and enjoy immediately.

Nutritional Information per Serving:

Calories: 281 |Fat: 16.6g|Sat Fat: 9g|Carbohydrates: 27.1g|Fiber: 0.2g|Sugar: 21.6g|Protein: 6.3g

Sweet Potato Pudding Gelato

Preparation Time: 10 minutes | Cooking Time: 3 minutes | Servings: 4

Ingredients:

4 large egg yolks

1 cup heavy cream

⅓ cup granulated sugar

½ of banana, peeled and sliced

½ cup frozen sweet potato, chopped

1 (3½-ounce) box cheesecake pudding mix

4 graham crackers, crumbled

Preparation:

1. In a small-sized saucepan, put in the egg yolks, heavy cream and sugar and whisk until blended thoroughly. 2. Place the saucepan on burner at around medium heat and cook for about 2-3 minutes, stirring continuously. 3. Take off the saucepan of egg mixture from burner and through a fine-mesh strainer, strain the blended mixture into an empty Ninja CREAMi pint container. 4. Place the container into an ice bath to cool. 5. After cooling, put in in the banana, sweet potato and pudding until blended thoroughly. 6. Cover the container with the storage lid and freeze for 24 hours. 7. After 24 hours, take off the lid from container and arrange into the outer bowl of Ninja CREAMi. 8. Install the "Creamerizer Paddle" onto the lid of outer bowl. 9. Then rotate the lid clockwise to lock. 10. Press "Power" button to turn on the unit. 11. Then press "GELATO" button. 12. When the program is completed, with a spoon, create a 1½-inch wide hole in the center that reaches the bottom of the pint container. 13. Put in crackers into the hole and press "MIX-IN" button. 14. When the program is completed, turn the outer bowl and release it from the machine. 15. Transfer the gelato into serving bowls and enjoy immediately.

Nutritional Information per Serving:

Calories: 404 |Fat: 17.1g|Sat Fat: 8.8g|Carbohydrates: 59.3g|Fiber: 2.6g|Sugar: 24.6g|Protein: 5g

Delicious Pistachio Gelato

Preparation Time: 10 minutes | Cooking Time: 3 minutes | Servings: 4

Ingredients:

4 large egg yolks
5 tablespoons granulated sugar
1 tablespoon honey
1 cup heavy cream

⅓ cup whole milk
1 teaspoon vanilla extract
⅓ cup pistachios, chopped

Preparation:

1. In a small-sized saucepan, put in the egg yolks, sugar and honey and whisk until blended thoroughly. 2. Put in heavy cream, milk and vanilla extract and whisk until blended thoroughly. 3. Place the saucepan on burner at around medium heat and cook for about 2-3 minutes, stirring continuously. 4. Take off the saucepan of milk mixture from burner and through a fine-mesh strainer, strain the blended mixture into an empty Ninja CREAMi pint container. 5. Place the container into an ice bath to cool. 6. After cooling, cover the container with the storage lid and freeze for 24 hours. 7. After 24 hours, take off the lid from container and arrange into the outer bowl of Ninja CREAMi. 8. Install the "Creamerizer Paddle" onto the lid of outer bowl. 9. Then rotate the lid clockwise to lock. 10. Press "Power" button to turn on the unit. 11. Then press "GELATO" button. 12. When the program is completed, with a spoon, create a 1½-inch wide hole in the center that reaches the bottom of the pint container. 13. Put in pistachios into the hole and press "MIX-IN" button. 14. When the program is completed, turn the outer bowl and release it from the machine. 15. Transfer the gelato into serving bowls and enjoy immediately.

Nutritional Information per Serving:

Calories: 271 |Fat: 18.6g|Sat Fat: 9.2g|Carbohydrates: 23.2g|Fiber: 0.5g|Sugar: 21g|Protein: 5g

Flavorful Pumpkin Gelato

Preparation Time: 10 minutes | Cooking Time: 3 minutes | Servings: 4

Ingredients:

3 large egg yolks
⅓ cup coconut sugar
1 tablespoon corn syrup
½ cup heavy cream
1 cup whole milk

½ cup pumpkin puree
½ teaspoon ground cinnamon
½ teaspoon ground nutmeg
¾ teaspoon vanilla extract

Preparation:

1. In a small-sized saucepan, put in the egg yolks, coconut sugar and b corn syrup and whisk until blended thoroughly. 2. Put in heavy cream, whole milk, pumpkin puree and spices and whisk until blended thoroughly. 3. Place the saucepan on burner at around medium heat and cook for about 2-3 minutes, stirring continuously. 4. Take off the pan of milk mixture from burner and blend in the vanilla extract. 5. Through a fine-mesh strainer, strain the blended mixture into an empty Ninja CREAMi pint container. 6. Place the container into an ice bath to cool. 7. After cooling, cover the container with the storage lid and freeze for 24 hours. 8. After 24 hours, take off the lid from container and arrange into the outer bowl of Ninja CREAMi. 9. Install the "Creamerizer Paddle" onto the lid of outer bowl. 10. Then rotate the lid clockwise to lock. 11. Press "Power" button to turn on the unit. 12. Then press "GELATO" button. 13. When the program is completed, turn the outer bowl and release it from the machine. 14. Transfer the gelato into serving bowls and enjoy immediately.

Nutritional Information per Serving:

Calories: 217 |Fat: 11.1g|Sat Fat: 5.9g|Carbohydrates: 26.2g|Fiber: 1.1g|Sugar: 21.8g|Protein: 4.7g

Peanut Gelato

Preparation Time: 15 minutes | Cooking Time: 9 minutes | Servings: 4

Ingredients:

1½ cups full-fat coconut milk

⅓ cup sugar

1 tablespoon cornstarch

3 tablespoons peanut butter

3 dark chocolate peanut butter cups, cut up

2 tablespoons peanuts, cut up

Preparation:

1. In a small-sized saucepan, put in coconut milk, sugar, and cornstarch on burner at around medium heat and whisk to incorporate. 2. Cook the mixture until boiling. 3. Immediately turn down the heat to low and cook for around 3-4 minutes. 4. Take off the pan of sugar mixture from burner and whisk in the peanut butter. 5. Transfer the mixture into an empty Ninja CREAMi pint container. 6. Place the container into an ice bath to cool. 7. After cooling, cover the container with the storage lid and freeze for 24 hours. 8. After 24 hours, take off the lid from container and arrange into the outer bowl of Ninja CREAMi. 9. Install the "Creamerizer Paddle" onto the lid of outer bowl. 10. Then rotate the lid clockwise to lock. 11. Press "Power" button to turn on the unit. 12. Then press "GELATO" button. 13. When the program is completed, with a spoon, create a 1½-inch wide hole in the center that reaches the bottom of the pint container. 14. Add the peanut butter cups and peanuts into the hole and press "MIX-IN" button. 15. When the program is completed, turn the outer bowl and release it from the machine. 16. Transfer the gelato into serving bowls and serve immediately.

Nutritional Information per Serving:

Calories: 450 |Fat: 34g|Sat Fat: 23.2g|Carbohydrates: 31.3g|Fiber: 1.1g|Sugar: 24.6g|Protein: 7.2g

Vanilla Gelato

Preparation Time: 10 minutes | Cooking Time: 5 minutes | Servings: 4

Ingredients:

1 cup whole milk

¾ cup heavy cream

2 egg yolks

⅓ cup granulated sugar

1 teaspoon vanilla bean paste

Preparation:

1. In a medium-sized saucepan, put in milk and remaining ingredients on burner at around medium heat and cook for around 5 minutes, whisking constantly. 2. Through a fine-mesh strainer, strain the mixture into an empty Ninja CREAMi pint container. 3. Place the container into an ice bath to cool. 4. After cooling, cover the container with the storage lid and freeze for 24 hours. 5. After 24 hours, take off the lid from container and arrange into the outer bowl of Ninja CREAMi. 6. Install the "Creamerizer Paddle" onto the lid of outer bowl. 7. Then rotate the lid clockwise to lock. 8. Press "Power" button to turn on the unit. 9. Then press "GELATO" button. 10. When the program is completed, turn the outer bowl and release it from the machine. 11. Transfer the gelato into serving bowls and serve immediately.

Nutritional Information per Serving:

Calories: 209 |Fat: 12.6g|Sat Fat: 7.1g|Carbohydrates: 21.6g|Fiber: 0g|Sugar: 21.2g|Protein: 3.8g

Fresh Raspberry Gelato

Preparation Time: 15 minutes Cooking Time: 10 minutes | Servings: 4

Ingredients:

1 cup whole milk

½ cup heavy cream

3 large egg yolks

⅓ cup granulated sugar

1 tablespoon honey

½ cup fresh raspberries, roughly chopped

Preparation:

1. In a medium-sized saucepan, put in milk and remaining ingredients except for raspberry pieces on burner at around medium heat. 2. Cook for around 7-10 minutes, whisking constantly. 3. Through a fine-mesh strainer, strain the blended mixture into an empty Ninja CREAMi pint container. 4. Place the container into an ice bath to cool. 5. After cooling, blend in the raspberry pieces. 6. Cover the container with the storage lid and freeze for 24 hours. 7. After 24 hours, take off the lid from container and arrange into the outer bowl of Ninja CREAMi. 8. Install the "Creamerizer Paddle" onto the lid of outer bowl. 9. Then rotate the lid clockwise to lock. 10. Press "Power" button to turn on the unit. 11. Then press "GELATO" button. 12. When the program is completed, turn the outer bowl and release it from the machine. 13. Transfer the gelato into serving bowls and enjoy immediately.

Nutritional Information per Serving:

Calories: 215 |Fat: 11g|Sat Fat: 5.8g|Carbohydrates: 26.5g|Fiber: 1g|Sugar: 25g|Protein: 4.5g

Tasty Sugar Cookies Gelato

Preparation Time: 10 minutes | Cooking Time: 5 minutes | Servings: 4

Ingredients:

1 cup whole milk

¾ cup heavy cream

⅓ cup granulated sugar

¼ cup sugar cookie mix

2 egg yolks

1 teaspoon vanilla extract

Preparation:

1. In a medium-sized saucepan, put in milk and remaining ingredients on burner at around medium heat and cook for around 5 minutes, whisking constantly. 2. Through a fine-mesh strainer, strain the blended mixture into an empty Ninja CREAMi pint container. 3. Pour the blended mixture into a Ninja Creami pint container, ensuring it does not go over the max fill line. 4. Place the container into an ice bath to cool. 5. After cooling, cover the container with the storage lid and freeze for 24 hours. 6. After 24 hours, take off the lid from container and arrange into the outer bowl of Ninja CREAMi. 7. Install the "Creamerizer Paddle" onto the lid of outer bowl. 8. Then rotate the lid clockwise to lock. 9. Press "Power" button to turn on the unit. 10. Then press "GELATO" button. 11. When the program is completed, turn the outer bowl and release it from the machine. 12. Transfer the gelato into serving bowls and enjoy immediately.

Nutritional Information per Serving:

Calories: 243 |Fat: 13.4g|Sat Fat: 7.3g|Carbohydrates: 27.8g|Fiber: 0g|Sugar: 24.1g|Protein: 4.1g

Cream Cheese Cacao Gelato

Preparation Time: 10 minutes | Cooking Time: 3 minutes | Servings: 4

Ingredients:

4 large egg yolks

¼ cup granulated sugar

2 tablespoons cacao powder

1 cup whole milk

⅓ cup heavy whipping cream

¼ cup cream cheese, softened

1 teaspoon vanilla extract

Preparation:

1. In a small-sized saucepan, put in the egg yolks, sugar and cacao powder and whisk until blended thoroughly. 2. Put in milk, heavy cream, cream cheese and vanilla extract and whisk until blended thoroughly. 3. Place the saucepan on burner at around medium heat and cook for about 2-3 minutes, stirring continuously. 4. Take off the saucepan of milk mixture from burner and through a fine-mesh strainer, strain the blended mixture into an empty Ninja CREAMi pint container. 5. Place the container into an ice bath to cool. 6. After cooling, cover the container with the storage lid and freeze for 24 hours. 7. After 24 hours, take off the lid from container and arrange into the outer bowl of Ninja CREAMi. 8. Install the "Creamerizer Paddle" onto the lid of outer bowl. 9. Then rotate the lid clockwise to lock. 10. Press "Power" button to turn on the unit. 11. Then press "GELATO" button. 12. When the program is completed, turn the outer bowl and release it from the machine. 13. Transfer the gelato into serving bowls and enjoy immediately.

Nutritional Information per Serving:

Calories: 232 |Fat: 15.8g|Sat Fat: 8.6g|Carbohydrates: 17.9g|Fiber: 0.8g|Sugar: 16g|Protein: 6.5g

Fresh Strawberry Gelato

Preparation Time: 15 minutes | Cooking Time: 10 minutes | Servings: 4

Ingredients:

1 cup whole milk

½ cup heavy cream

3 large egg yolks

⅓ cup granulated sugar

1 tablespoon corn syrup

½ cup fresh strawberries, quartered

Preparation:

1. In a medium-sized saucepan, put in milk and remaining ingredients except for strawberries on burner at around medium heat and cook for around 7-10 minutes, whisking constantly. 2. Through a fine-mesh strainer, strain the mixture into an empty Ninja CREAMi pint container. 3. Place the container into an ice bath to cool. 4. After cooling, stir in the strawberry pieces. 5. Cover the container with the storage lid and freeze for 24 hours. 6. After 24 hours, take off the lid from container and arrange into the outer bowl of Ninja CREAMi. 7. Install the "Creamerizer Paddle" onto the lid of outer bowl. 8. Then rotate the lid clockwise to lock. 9. Press "Power" button to turn on the unit. 10. Then press "GELATO" button. 11. When the program is completed, turn the outer bowl and release it from the machine. 12. Transfer the gelato into serving bowls and serve immediately.

Nutritional Information per Serving:

Calories: 210 |Fat: 11g|Sat Fat: 5.8g|Carbohydrates: 25.3g|Fiber: 0.4g|Sugar: 22.1g|Protein: 4.4g

Conclusion

The Ninja Creami is a fantastic kitchen gadget that makes it easy to enjoy handmade frozen delights. It enables you to make a range of delicious sweets and snacks in the convenience of your own home because to its cutting-edge technology, simplicity of use, and customization choices.

The Creami differs from conventional techniques in that it can accelerate and streamline the freezing process. Long waits and difficult procedures are no longer necessary. You can enjoy creamy ice creams, zingy sorbets, decadent milkshakes, and more quickly and easily with the Creami.

Both novice and expert cooks can use the gadget thanks to its simple design and simple controls. To effortlessly produce customised frozen treats that suit your tastes, simply choose the desired settings, experiment with flavours, and add your preferred mix-ins.

The Creami also offers flexibility in terms of functionality and capacity. There is a Creami model to suit your needs, whether you want to prepare smaller batches for small parties or larger ones for large ones. Some versions also come with extra capabilities that let you make non-frozen desserts or combinations, broadening your range of culinary options.

The majority of the Creami's parts are dishwasher-safe or simple to hand-wash, making cleaning and maintaining it a snap. This guarantees convenience and longevity, enabling you to take pleasure in the performance of the appliance for many years to come.

You may unleash your imagination and discover countless possibilities in the frozen desserts world with the Ninja Creami. It gives you the freedom to play around with flavours, textures, and ingredients, transforming your kitchen into a paradise for desserts. The thrill of handmade frozen indulgence is here to replace store-bought goodies.

In conclusion, the Ninja Creami makes creating frozen treats quick, easy, and versatile while providing a pleasurable experience that will satisfy your cravings and dazzle your loved ones. Prepare to travel a tasty path of frozen treats with the Ninja Creami by your side.

Appendix 1 Measurement Conversion Chart

WEIGHT EQUIVALENTS

US STANDARD	METRIC (APPROXINATE)
1 ounce	28 g
2 ounces	57 g
5 ounces	142 g
10 ounces	284 g
15 ounces	425 g
16 ounces (1 pound)	455 g
1.5pounds	680 g
2pounds	907 g

VOLUME EQUIVALENTS (DRY)

US STANDARD	METRIC (APPROXIMATE)
⅛ teaspoon	0.5 mL
¼ teaspoon	1 mL
½ teaspoon	2 mL
¾ teaspoon	4 mL
1 teaspoon	5 mL
1 tablespoon	15 mL
¼ cup	59 mL
½ cup	118 mL
¾ cup	177 mL
1 cup	235 mL
2 cups	475 mL
3 cups	700 mL
4 cups	1 L

TEMPERATURES EQUIVALENTS

FAHRENHEIT(F)	CELSIUS (C) (APPROXIMATE)
225 °F	107 °C
250 °F	120 °C
275 °F	135 °C
300 °F	150 °C
325 °F	160 °C
350 °F	180 °C
375 °F	190 °C
400 °F	205 °C
425 °F	220 °C
450 °F	235 °C
475 °F	245 °C
500 °F	260 °C

VOLUME EQUIVALENTS (LIQUID)

US STANDARD	US STANDARD (OUNCES)	METRIC (APPROXIMATE)
2 tablespoons	1 fl.oz	30 mL
¼ cup	2 fl.oz	60 mL
½ cup	4 fl.oz	120 mL
1 cup	8 fl.oz	240 mL
1½ cup	12 fl.oz	355 mL
2 cups or 1 pint	16 fl.oz	475 mL
4 cups or 1 quart	32 fl.oz	1 L
1 gallon	128 fl.oz	4 L

Appendix 2 Recipes Index

Made in United States
Orlando, FL
18 December 2024

56053769R00064